MW00988387

CAROLE MAYHALL is the wife of Jack, who is United States director of The Navigators. They are the parents of one daughter, Lynn, who is married to a Navigator representative and involved in a university ministry in Mexico.

Carole graduated from high school in a small town in southern Michigan, and from Wheaton College (Illinois) with a degree in Christian Education. She served as the education director for an Ohio church before she married Jack.

With her husband, Carole has lived and ministered in various situations and communities from Virginia to California and from Minnesota to Georgia. Since joining the Navigator staff, the Mayhalls have spoken at seminars and conferences around the world. Carole is a frequent speaker at women's gatherings and has held seminars not only in the United States, but also in Europe and Japan.

When asked what she finds most rewarding about speaking and ministering, she replies, "I love to teach and see God turn a light on for someone. I love to see God meet people's specific needs. When that happens, it is a real thrill to me.

"My mother was always helping other people. Seeing her willingness to help and her heart for others, has motivated me to go into the ministry I presently have."

Carole and Jack are the authors of *Marriage Takes More Than Love* (NavPress, 1978). Carole has also written *Lord, Teach Me Wisdom* (NavPress, 1979) and *Lord of My Rocking Boat* (NavPress, 1981.)

FROM THE HEART OF A WOMAN

CAROLE MAYHALL

NAVPRESS

A MINISTRY OF THE NAVIGATORS
P.O. Box 6000, Colorado Springs, Colorado 80934

The Navigators is an international, evangelical
Christian organization. Jesus Christ gave His
followers the Great Commission to go and
make disciples (Matthew 28:19). The aim of
The Navigators is to help fulfill that commission by multiplying laborers for Christ in
every nation.

NavPress is the publishing ministry of The
Navigators. NavPress publications are tools to
help Christians grow. Although publications
alone cannot make disciples or change lives,
they can help believers learn biblical
discipleship, and apply what they learn to
their lives and ministries.

© 1976 by The Navigators
All rights reserved, including translation
Library of Congress Catalog Card Number:
   76-24066
ISBN: 0-89109-421-0
14217

Ninth printing, 1982

Printed in the United States of America

CONTENTS

Foreword   9

Preface   10

1. The Yearning Heart   13

2. The Growing Heart   18

3. The Reflecting Heart   23

4. The Praying Heart   33

5. The Listening Heart   39

6. The Applying Heart   45

7. The Expanding Heart   50

   Interlude: Poems of Prayer   61

8. The Searching Heart   69

9. The Joyful Heart   76

10. The Happy Heart   85

11. The Yielded Heart   92

12. The Wounded Heart   97

13. The Heart of Beauty   102

DEDICATION

To my husband, Jack, without whom I am not complete—my best friend, companion and encourager on the Journey

To our daughter, Lynn, and her husband, Tim, who continually rejoice my heart

To Mother, whose life is a song and an inspiration, and Dad, who showed me the way to heaven before going there

To Mom and Dad Mayhall, radiant with Him

I affectionately dedicate this book.

ACKNOWLEDGEMENTS

Without the help, encouragement, suggestions and critiquing of Monte Unger, I might never have finished this book. I owe him much.

Without The Navigators, whose principles of multiplication, practical help and study are incorporated in this book, I would have had no story to tell.

Without individual Navigators, Skip and Buzzie Gray, who initially touched our lives, Bob and Marion Foster, who continued to instruct us, and uncounted others along the way, I might not have found Reality.

To all of these, and many others, who have inspired, helped and been used in my life, I am deeply grateful.

FOREWORD

This book is from the heart of a woman who has tasted the depths of sorrow and despair, and has come forth triumphant. She is a person who has been refreshingly honest from her earliest childhood, and here she bares some of the very personal lessons of her life.

I was reminded anew that God has a divine plan for each of our lives. Regardless of the price we often have to pay, we must not miss it. At times the Christian life is not easy, but as we "let go and let God" work in and through us, it becomes one glorious journey. That is what Carole shares with us.

God runs a costly school. Many of His lessons are spelled out through tears and deep heartaches. Since He is the Chairman of the Board in our lives, our wills must become "not my will, but Thine be done." When we do that, we truly bear the fruit of the Spirit.

Carole has learned through the years to go to God's living Word for all of life's "dailies," for He is our *only* hope. And she has so beautifully shared that *He,* our Lord and Saviour, keeps His word and makes something beautiful out of our lives for His honor and glory and praise.

Carole's life is truly that of Proverbs 31:10-31—a woman who dares to believe God all the way home.

LILA M. TROTMAN

PREFACE

Tears formed beneath my lashes. I blinked quickly. It wouldn't help to cry.

The rain was lessening now. A drip, somewhere distant in the house, slowed and stopped.

I glanced around the bedroom. The rug had been pulled up, exposing the concrete floor. Shoes from the closet overflowed the bed onto the chair. My husband, Jack, slumped in a chair near my own.

There we sat. Dejected. Discouraged. Muscles aching. Eyes red from staying up most of the night fighting rising water in our home from the second torrential rain in two months. Our home had looked like a disaster area those weeks as we tried to undo the damage from the previous flooding. We had spent more money than we could afford to fix the problem, only to discover two months later that the problem was, in fact, *not* solved!

We were beat, and felt beaten at the same time.

I looked at my husband and asked, "What do you suppose God is trying to teach us? There must be some lesson in all of this."

Jack agreed. One thing was apparent to both of us. We didn't want to give this kind of work, effort, money, thought and energy on a *house*. There were too many more important matters to give ourselves to.

As we considered the situation, we felt that this was God's way of reminding us that we needed to reevaluate all of our activities in the light of who we are and where we are going— to rethink time spent with our life-goals in mind.

I was reminded of a quote by George Bernard Shaw who said, "We seem not to live long enough to take our lives seriously."

Daily I live with two fears—healthy fears if there are such things. The first is that I would cause defeat or discourage-

10

ment in the lives of my husband or my daughter. Christ said, "It is inevitable that stumbling blocks come; but woe to that man through whom the stumbling block comes!" (Matthew 18:7) It is a frightening thing to think of being that stumbling block.

My second fear is that I will miss something God has for me in this life. And it is mind-expanding to contemplate *all* that *He wants me to have.* I don't want to be robbed of even one of God's riches by not taking the time to let Him invade my life. By not listening to what He is telling me. By allowing the routine, pressing matters of my minutes bankrupt me of time for the most exciting, most fulfilling relationship in life.

I want to grow . . . and expand . . . and explode with His joy. I want my heart to overflow with His love. I want to feel like the psalmist as he says, "You [God] have endowed him [man] with eternal happiness. You have given him the unquenchable *joy* of Your presence" (Psalm 21:6, LB).

J. B. Phillips paraphrases Paul beautifully: "Base your happiness on your hope in Christ" (Romans 12:12, PH). How often I fail to do this. I base my happiness on my husband's love, my child developing properly, security, an interesting trip, friends. Have you ever eagerly looked forward to a trip and then felt a vague uneasiness during the entire journey? You are disturbed because you feel like something is missing? At times like this I remember that the only way to deep joy is in basing my happiness in Christ *alone.*

That evening as we sat in our soggy bedroom, contemplating what was really important in our lives, God gave us a new determination to give our lives only to the *best.* But how is this possible? How do I really maintain a life that is based in Christ *alone?*

The great majority of Jesus' miracles were complete and instantaneous. One notable exception is found in the incident with the blind man at Bethsaida (Mark 8:22-25). He was brought to Jesus and the Lord was asked to touch him. But instead of healing him there before the crowd, Jesus took him by the hand and led him out of the village. Then He put saliva on his eyes. Finally He laid His hands on the blind man and asked, "Do you see anything?"

This man must have been facing Christ in order for his eyes to be touched in this manner. His reply was, "I see *men,* but they are like trees walking about."

The poor man was seeing double. His vision was blurred and distorted.

Again Jesus placed His hands on the man's eyes and as Mark states, "He looked intently and was restored, and began to see everything clearly" (8:25).

Many times I have felt like that man at Bethsaida. When I tried to look at Jesus, I couldn't see Him clearly. I desperately wanted His complete restoration, but my vision was distorted. I wanted to look intently, but my spiritual sight was blurred.

Nearly 20 years ago God began a process in my life through which He is . . .

- teaching me to look intently
- restoring me daily
- clearing my vision to see Him distinctly

This book is written with the prayer that some of God's methods of touching me may help you be touched by Him.

The Yearning Heart/1

Our car snaked up the mountain, the U-Haul swishing behind. Our one-year-old daughter, crowded in among her toys, played happily in the back seat. Mount Shasta, capped with January snows and brilliant in the winter sun, loomed before us.

We were headed north and I was excited. I was also apprehensive.

We were going to a strange part of the country. A new job. A totally different situation. At the moment, my mood was as exuberant as the sunlight which danced on the stream playing hide-n-seek with the road. As we drove down the other side of the mountain, however, we descended into a cloudbank, and didn't see the sun again for three months.

The windshield wipers beat in hypnotic rhythm as the clouds enveloped us. As I peered through the grey mist, memories of past years washed over me.

* * *

"The Bible lives here" was not a plaque hung in the large old kitchen of the home in which I was raised. But it was written in the lives of my parents and read by my brother, sister and me, and many others who paraded in and out of our lives.

I would read it when my mother, with tears still wet on her cheeks, came out of her bedroom after talking with God. I saw it in my father, a comforting, solid man who lived the Christian life more than he talked about it.

I saw Christ in them, but He wasn't real to me. I knew God answered their prayer requests, but I sometimes wondered if the answers I was seeing to my prayers were really only because they had prayed too. Somehow I didn't experience the *feeling* that God was right there with me. Two areas caused me special concern.

One was my temper. As a child, even before I could talk, I would have a temper tantrum and hold my breath till I turned blue in the face. The doctor relieved Mom's fears on that one; he said that if I really did hold my breath long enough to lose consciousness, I would automatically start to breathe again.

Later, when I could talk, I would get so violently angry as to lose all control—hitting my head against the wall and striking out at anyone who came near me. I seemed to have no control at all over my anger. I became afraid of what I might do some day in a literal "fit of rage."

Second, I had been taught that someday Jesus Christ would come again to this earth to take His children with Him to heaven. His *children*. When I was 12, I began to realize that God has no grandchildren. If I wasn't His child by adoption into His family, I would have no part of Him. I reasoned that when He came back for His family, I would be left behind.

In Sunday School, I had learned the verse, "For with a

shout, with the voice of the archangel and the trumpet of God, the Lord Himself will descend from heaven, and those who died in Christ will rise first. Afterward we, the living who remain, will be caught up along with them in the clouds to meet the Lord in the air. And so we shall forever be with the Lord" (I Thessalonians 4:16, 17, BERK).

In my imagination, I could picture the Lord returning in just that way. My mother and father and a great many people I knew and loved would suddenly be gone. I would be left behind. I would be alone.

Occasionally, fear would descend with the night, closing tightly around me. I would lie very still, straining to hear nightsounds from the house—the creaking of springs from my parents' room, the gentle snores of my father, someone moving softly about. If all was still, my feet would reach down to the cold wooden floor and, with pounding heart, I would creep into my parents' bedroom. I would make my eyes into tiny slits so I could quickly shut out the world if I found their great old-fashioned bed empty.

I knew that God loved me, that the estrangement and fear I was feeling wasn't *His* doing. He had paid a tremendous price in order to forgive me: His Son had died so that I might become His adopted child. His *love* made Him willing to leave heaven. His *love* was the reason He suffered so for me. It was because of His *love* that He was willing to pay the penalty for my wrongdoings.

Yet it was the *fear* of missing out on that great love which finally drew me into His family.

One night I knew I could not live another hour with that fear, so I poured out my despair to my mother. She simply told me that all I had to do to become God's child was to ask Jesus into my heart. His Word states it clearly: "As many as received Him, to them gave He power to become the sons of God" (John 1:12, KJV). I knew that meant daughters too.

I knelt with mother in my bedroom and asked Jesus to come into my life.

I am convinced He did just that for a number of reasons. Two stand out: I never had another temper tantrum that was uncontrollable (though I still struggle with anger), and I was never afraid again that the Lord would come and leave me behind.

In the next few years, I matured physically to an adult. My growth spiritually, however, was characterized by spurts of development, complete stops and sometimes a slide backwards.

That God *was,* I could not doubt. When I was 14, one outstanding proof convinced me of that.

My mother had been hospitalized for three weeks following serious surgery, when one Saturday, for the first time in my life, I saw my father cry.

"The doctors just told me that your mother is dying," Dad told me. "She has had sinking spells every few hours and once her heart stopped completely. They don't expect her to last much longer."

I was thunderstruck. It was a blow my mind could not accept.

The next morning was cloudy and dark, an exact reflection of my mood. I walked the streets of our town, crying inside.

"God," I begged. "I can't stand it. Please don't let Mom die. I need her. Daddy needs her. We all need her . . . and I can't bear not knowing if You *are* going to heal her. So, please tell me if You will let her stay. Show me now. Somehow."

I was stuck. How could I ask God to show me? I looked at the thick, black clouds overhead, then blurted out, "Lord, if You are going to heal Mom, then, please, just let the sun break through the clouds."

For one brief, brilliant moment, the clouds parted and the sun flooded the world. Then the rift closed.

But I *knew.*

Three days later, while a group of teenagers knelt on a frayed blue carpet in our living room, the phone rang. Daddy's joyful voice came over the wire, "The crisis has passed. Mother will be OK."

Could I doubt that God *was?*

In my home, in a small wood-frame church, and on the spacious, shady campus of a Christian college, I learned truths about God. But my vision of Him somehow remained blurred. An occasional vital touch on my life made me critically aware of what I was missing. But how was I to touch God daily? Or, like that blind man at Bethsaida, how was I to have *Him* touch *me?*

I read the Bible, but often with a yawn.

I experienced answered prayer, but rarely was God involved in the "dailies" of my life.

I knew somewhere, somehow, *there had to be more.*

I longed for a brand new walk with God.

I wanted to close the door of mediocrity and open the door of "life on a miracle plane."

I seemed to be stretching . . . reaching . . . straining to clutch reality, only to grasp air.

* * *

A turn in the highway brought me back to the reality of the present. Portland, the Northwest's "City of Roses," focused in before us. What lay ahead? I was the wife of a youth director and mother of a year-old baby girl. One part of me was a happy, contented wife and mother. Another part of me was frustrated and dissatisfied. Continually the yearning cry of my heart was, "Touch me. Oh, touch me, Lord God."

All He needed was to be asked.

The Growing Heart/2

Jack has the red hair and I have the temper.

The first five years of our marriage were volatile. Our clashes frequent. It is true that marital happiness is won through conflict, as David Augsburger points out, "Even conflict about conflicts." The secret of marital success lies in knowing how to *handle* differences, a knowledge we did not then have. Failure lay close to the surface of our marriage.

Basically, I knew that it was my job to make Jack happy, and God's job to make him good. But somehow I felt that God needed my help.

A pattern was emerging in our relationship. When Jack would say or do something I didn't like, my anger was ignited. I punished him with cold silence, then expressed myself with venom and hostility. Our emotions spent, one of us would apologize and the quarrel was forgotten—till next time.

But these eruptions were becoming more and more frequent, and *nothing was changing.*

We recognized this. We even talked about it. We just didn't know what to *do* about it. And this wormed its way into our domestic peace of mind.

At the same time, a problem in our work caused growing concern. Working with youth in a church is at the same time challenging, frustrating, delightful, discouraging, disturbing, creative and rewarding. One thing it is not: boring.

We loved it. And the kids we ministered to were responding in growing numbers. And that was our problem: Too much to do; too little time in which to do it.

We definitely needed help—more adult leadership which was godly, innovative and mature. Also willing.

A few in the church were giving unbelievable effort and time to the work; the majority, little or nothing. Leadership training classes drew only the ones already loaded down with responsibilities. The question plagued us: How could we inspire and train more people to help others?

We had no answer to this vital question.

Then, in an inauspicious manner, a chain of events began that changed our lives and brought solutions to these difficulties.

Shortly after we moved to Portland, a friend asked Jack to a conference in a nearby city. My husband reluctantly agreed to drive down for one Saturday morning, and that one small decision, grudgingly made, changed the entire course of our lives.

At the conference, several men spoke briefly after the main message. Men with diverse occupations—a businessman, a student, a pastor, a military man. Different personalities and widely separated walks of life, but essentially they had one message.

Each man had led a person to Christ. Then in a systematic, sensitive way had "fathered" the new Christian, helping him take those first wobbly steps in the Christian life. But the help didn't stop when the steps became more sure. He was nurtured till his walk was stronger and steadier—till finally he could stand and walk on his own to become a mature follower of Christ.

There was more. The tools for growth were so workable that the ones who had been helped were able to show *others* how to find Christ. And in the same systematic and sensitive way help them with their walk toward maturity in Christ. It was a multiplication process, an exploding principle of growth.

Jack thought he saw a glimmer of light through the fog. Might not this be a way to inspire and train people in the church to help our young people?

As Jack drove back that Saturday afternoon, he had a conversation with himself. He said, "Suppose I had a brand new Christian sitting here who really wanted to grow into a mature Christian. What would I tell him? How would I help him personally? What would I want him to know and do to *insure* that he would grow up in Christ?"

The key word was to *insure* his growth. Jack's current method was at best haphazard. At worst, a failure. The present operational procedure was to get a new Christian involved in as many church activities as possible and then . . . hope! Some grew; some didn't.

Suddenly Jack realized that he would run out of things to tell that new Christian in less than one hour. With a college and seminary education, he did not have the know-how needed to help *one* individual walk toward God. He probably *had* the knowledge wafting around somewhere in the recesses of his mind, but to translate it into a practical plan was something else again. He knew he needed help.

God did not keep him waiting long. A young man, Skip Gray, spoke to our college group the next week. He brought a simple yet profound message. All of us easily understood and grasped it, and began to realize its powerful implications.

Skip spoke on practical ways to take the Word of God into a life. He had never been to seminary, yet the skillful way he used the Bible and how he related it personally to life impressed both of us. So Jack asked him to lunch.

For four years my husband had been to a seminary that taught him every book of the Bible in either Greek, Hebrew or English. He knew eschatology, exegesis and ecclesiology. He could tell you all about hermeneutics and soteriology. He could have easily disregarded anything the younger non-seminarian would say or could teach him.

But that day Jack became a learner. And he has remained a learner to this day.

Solomon wrote:

> My son, if you will accept my words, and store up my commandments within you, so that you make your ear attend to wisdom, and your heart reach out for discernment;
> yes, if you beseech understanding, and lift your voice for discernment;
> if you seek her as silver, and search for her as for hidden treasures;
> then you will understand reverence of the Lord and find the knowledge of God.
> For the Lord gives wisdom; from His mouth come knowledge and discernment (Proverbs 2:1-6, BERK).

During the next four intensive months, my husband tapped Skip's practical knowledge. They spent every available minute of their free time together. I must admit that I wondered what they could find to talk about all that time. My first thought was, *Oh, well, he'll get tired of all of this soon. I can wait it out.*

As the days gave birth to weeks, then months, jealousy of all the time my husband *wasn't* spending with me gnawed a gaping hole in my patience.

Jack desperately wanted to learn how to insure spiritual growth in one individual. But quietly, he was learning to know God in a deeper way than ever before. I didn't know it then, but the first person this was going to affect was me.

The Reflecting Heart / 3

One evening, two months after the luncheon, Jack came home and shouted from the front door, "Hi, honey. How's everything?"

He was greeted with silence. Then, reluctantly, a cold voice answered from the kitchen and I said, "Oh, fine."

Only it wasn't fine. And by the icicles frosting my tone, he could tell that with certainty.

"What's the matter?" he queried, coming into the kitchen.

"Nothing," was my flat-toned response.

"I can tell something's bothering you. What is it?" he persisted.

This was exactly what I had hoped he would do. In fact, I would have gotten worse and worse if he hadn't kept asking. We had been married long enough for him to have figured *that* one out!

So whatever had been simmering on the back burner of my anger all day boiled over.

This was our usual pattern. But something different

happened that evening for which I was totally unprepared. Instead of coming back at me with disgust or a quick retort, Jack just looked at me with love and tenderness. He said, "Maybe you are right. Let's pray about it together."

At first I was astonished. Then flustered. Finally, ashamed. I felt like washing myself right down the drain.

We did pray about it . . . or rather Jack did. I couldn't get a word past my confusion.

Like a physical blow, it struck me that God was doing something real in Jack's life. This was not his normal response to my anger. I suddenly realized that if I didn't let God communicate His truth to me in a deep way, Jack and I soon wouldn't be on spiritual speaking terms.

That isn't the purest motivation for letting God do a work in a life, but God loved me so much that He was willing to use *any* motivation to get me to listen.

God had changed something in Jack's attitude. Of that I was certain. But how? I sensed that it might have something to do with the Scripture he had been memorizing lately, but I wasn't sure. Later I found out that Jack had been ready to blast a quick retort, when a verse he had just memorized stopped him. It was: "For ye have need of patience, that after ye have done the will of God, ye might receive the promise" (Hebrews 10:36, KJV). It was slightly out of context in the Bible, but definitely in the context of this quarrel.

Till that evening, I had wanted no part of a project of memorizing Scripture. It seemed like a whole lot of hard work that I didn't need to keep me busy. I had memorized Scripture for Sunday School, which I thought was the *proper* time and place for it.

But now I was an adult. The wife of a youth director. Memorizing Scripture simply had no valid appeal to me. I could see no reason to discipline myself to do this. But a reason had just exploded in my face.

Later I heard it said, "I used to memorize Scripture, but now I *learn it by heart.*"

I like that. I began that very week to "learn it by heart," and it was one of the most astonishing methods God used to begin to change my character. I often say, "Don't memorize Scripture unless you want God to change your life," because He will do just that as you absorb His Word into your heart.

Amazing things began to happen. Some I liked. Some hurt. Though I knew there were many areas of my personality that needed drastic surgery, the cutting process was painful.

One sunny afternoon, a small group had met for prayer. We were drinking our second cup of coffee and discussing the requests for which we wanted to pray.

"Well," I sighed, "I wish you'd pray for Sue. She's having trouble with her marriage. Her husband is really edgy lately and . . . " I almost strangled on the next phrase. Because straight out of heaven, or so it seemed to me, God's voice intoned on my soul, "Carole [He gets very personal with me], 'A talebearer reveals secrets, but he who is trustworthy conceals a matter' " (Proverbs 11:13).

Later, I could laugh about the incident. Reading II Timothy 3:16, 17, I found that God uses His Word for teaching, for reproof, for correction and instruction. Without a doubt, I had just been thoroughly reproved.

On another occasion, Lynn, our daughter, came bursting in the door. "Mom" she wailed, "Nancy won't play with me. She says I'm bossy and make her do the things I want to and . . . " I turned the volume way down on my listening device and only half-heard the remaining monolog. An answer had already formed in my mind.

From Proverbs 18:2 God's Sword very pointedly poked. "Carole, 'A fool does not delight in understanding, but only in revealing his own mind.' "

I sank to the floor beside Lynn, my mental recorder already intensified. I *listened* . . . and *heard* her before I spoke.

This verse continues to be a great help to me in teaching me to be a sensitive listener, an attribute lacking in my impatient nature. God is faithful in reminding me to listen carefully to those around me.

Lessons continue every day. Recently, Jack was overseas and his letters weren't reaching me regularly. My vivid imagination conjured up all sorts of awful things, not the least of which was, "He just doesn't care that I am here all alone and missing him so. He just doesn't love me the way I love him."

As I was indulging in the world's worst indoor sport—feeling sorry for myself—the Holy Spirit spoke from a freshly memorized verse. "If you love someone you will be loyal to him no matter what the cost. You will always believe in him, always expect the best of him, and always stand your ground in defending him" (I Corinthians 13:7, LB).

"Help me, Lord," I prayed . "Forgive me. Cleanse these negative thoughts from my mind. Please guard my imagination."

As God's Word was made available to my heart, I found God changing my habits, thoughts and desires. The times I needed power from the Word most were generally times I didn't care to look for a verse. The answer had to be readily available for God's Spirit to use in my life, sometimes like a comforting hand, or at other times like a sword; yes, sometimes even like a hammer, and I needed to be hit over the head with it!

I began a systematic memory course and learned two or three verses with their references each week. I found it helped me remember the "address" of a verse if I quoted the verse with the reference before and after I said it aloud. I also discovered that the initial memorizing of a verse was a great deal easier than the retention of it.

I have heard it said that many of us spend almost seven years of our lives just *waiting*. As I thought about all the times I had waited for the doctor, the dentist, a friend to arrive, the dinner to be cooked, and all sorts of other things, I concluded that in my case it might even be *more* than seven years. What spiritual wealth I might accumulate if I could buy up all that wasted "waiting time."

So I began to carry those verses around with me, written out on small cards so that I could go over them during the times I was riding in the car, ironing, even vacuuming, as well as those periods of waiting that were so common. And, as I was reviewing these verses, I couldn't help but really *think* about them.

It was while concentrating on learning and reviewing these passages that I discovered the truth of Proverbs 23:7, "As [a man] thinks within himself, so he is."

I have one of these wild, maverick imaginations which I sometimes wish could be traded in on an old steady plowhorse. My thoughts can race from a doctor's appointment or an ache in my arm to a deathbed scene in which I am the central figure. I'll be driving down the street alone in the car, tears streaming down my cheeks as I think about this dismal picture.

What a waste of time. And imagination.

It is God who gave us our minds—our abilities to imagine, to reason, to think. He gave these to us so that we might honor Him.

Often I don't use this gift. I abuse it. Knowing this, as I was driving alone one day on a two hour trip, I determined to meditate on a passage of Scripture in a systematic way. I had heard of a method which I could remember by the letters **A E I O U**. That morning I experimented with this method of meditation, and what a difference it made on that trip and in my life thereafter.

Psalm 23 seemed like a good Scripture to start. The process works like this:

A is *ask questions.*

That psalm begins, "The Lord is my shepherd." I asked myself questions about that phrase such as: In what *way* is He my shepherd? (That took 15 minutes right there!) *When* do I experience Him as my shepherd?

I experienced Christ most often as Shepherd in the way He guided and protected me.

Shortly before this meditation, a cloudburst had deluged our area just as I delivered Lynn to a church party about 30 minutes from our home. Starting back, I prayed for guidance whether to go the way I had come—the freeway— or to go back a longer way. God seemed to indicate that the freeway should be avoided.

That was one of the scariest drives of my life. Streets were flooded. My brakes got wet, making it difficult to stop the car; lawns were on fire from downed power lines, sending sparks crackling into the streets; electricity was out over most of the city, making vision even more difficult through the driving rain. I wondered if the car—a totally unreliable vehicle—would stop altogether.

Because many streets were completely blocked by flooding, I had to go miles out of my way to get home. I finally arrived, exhausted and teary, two hours later. But the Scripture that kept sustaining me on the whole trip was, "When thou passest through the waters, I will be with thee; and through the rivers, they shall not overflow thee" (Isaiah 43:2, KJV).

A news item on the front page of the paper the next day told of a woman and her 12-year-old daughter who had attempted the very underpass which led on to the freeway that I would have taken—*at the exact time I would have taken it.* They had driven into 12 feet of water and a passing motorist had to rescue them from their submerged vehicle.

Yes, I had experienced God as my guiding Shepherd, caring for me in very specific ways, on many occasions.

"I shall not want." What does this really mean? Will I never want anything? In what areas have I already experienced this? How is He my sufficiency from want? Did you ever meditate on the beautiful fact that the more you experience Christ, the less you'll want of anything else? He has said that He is the great I AM with the power to be ALL that we need. Do I need peace? He *is* peace. Do I need security? He *is* security. Whatever my need may be, He becomes the answer to that need completely.

On that terrifying drive through the rain, I needed several things. I needed strength not to get hysterical. I needed inward peace to keep me secure. I needed protection and help just to get *home.* God not only took care of these needs, but gave me the great assurance that He was right there in the car with me. Sometimes I know this in my head, but don't feel it in my *heart.* That night I needed to *feel* His presence. And I did.

When I came to the phrase, "Thy rod and Thy staff they comfort me," I was really puzzled. I'd never given it a thought before, but I began to contemplate how God's rod, an instrument of chastening and guidance, was a comfort. To me, it seemed like the rod would be full of fear, and not a comfort. If God had to use His rod on me, it would be for discipline.

One definition of meditation is that it is "mental Bible study," and I really grappled with that one phrase. But God and I were grappling together as I prayed and thought about

God's discipline. And the mental lightswitch flipped on. Yes, discipline in love *is* a comfort. What a relief it is to know that a loving Father will reach out with His rod to stop me *before* I fall over the cliff of disobedience. He gives me a free will to disobey, but He will do everything apart from violating that free will to keep me on the right path. And that *is* a comfort.

E is *emphasize words.*

I took each word of the verse separately and gave emphasis to it, thinking about the importance of that particular word.

THE Lord is my shepherd—there is only one Lord.

The **LORD** is my shepherd—He is the Lord of lords and King of kings.

The Lord **IS** my shepherd—what surety!

The Lord is **MY** shepherd—how personal. How precious.

The Lord is my **SHEPHERD**—He cares for me as His own lamb.

I is *illustrate.*

A five-year-old girl was taught this verse by using the five fingers on her hand for each word. She would touch each and say, "*The* (touching her thumb) *Lord* (index finger) *is* (middle) *my* (fourth) *shepherd* (little finger)." One day she became ill and didn't recover. Her mother found her with one little hand hanging on tightly to the fourth finger of her other hand. "The Lord is MY shepherd" she had been saying as she met her Shepherd face to face.

O is *other Scriptures.*

My mind reflected on John 10:11; Jesus said, "I am the Good Shepherd; the Good Shepherd lays down His life for the sheep." He wouldn't *do* anything or *allow* anything to come into my life that would not be right and good for me, because He is the *good* Shepherd. He also said that His sheep hear His voice (John 10:27). I took some time praying about that one, because so often my ears are stuffed with self and His voice is faint and far away.

U is *use*.

How can I really use this in my life? At this point in my thinking God had already brought so many needs to mind, it was a matter of sorting out which one He wanted me to work on first. I felt like the sheep described in a poem:

> Lord You know
> I'm such a stupid sheep.
> I worry
> about all sorts of things
> whether I'll find grazing land
> still cool water
> a fold at night
> in which I can feel safe.
> I don't.
> I only find troubles
> want
> loss.
> I turn aside from You
> to plan my rebel way.
> I go astray.
> I follow other shepherds
> even other stupid sheep.
> Then when I end up
> on some dark mountain
> cliffs before
> wild animals behind
> I start to bleat
> Shepherd Shepherd

find me save me
or I die.
And You do.

(Joseph Bayly, *Psalms of My Life*)

That two-hour drive was a real delight. It started a concentrated effort on my part to control my thoughts rather than letting my thoughts control me. Paul talks about "taking every thought captive to the obedience of Christ" (II Corinthians 10:5), and this simple method of meditation helped me do this.

In many of our waking hours, our minds are of necessity occupied with routine matters. We do have to plan supper, make telephone calls, check our Christmas lists. However there must be many minutes, even hours of our days, that we spend with our minds drifting. If we can give this drift direction, by methodically and prayerfully dwelling on Christ through His Words, we could open the shutters to see unknown vistas. Paul commands, *"Set* your mind on things above, not on the things that are on earth" (Colossians 3:2).

I found meditation to be a practical way to "look to Jesus."*

---

*In his book *Meditation: The Bible Tells You How* (NavPress, 1976), Jim Downing has written extensively about methods of meditation that really work.

The Praying Heart/4

As I reached the corner, the bus disappeared down the street.

I stood looking after it, helpless and frustrated. Irritated with the baby sitter who had been late. Put-out with the doctor two transfers away who waited for no one and charged the patient if an appointment was missed. Thwarted by the bus driver who kept that dumb bus on time.

Then I thought, *Wait a minute! I wonder if God is interested in my getting to that doctor's on time? Is this something I can pray about? Well, it can't hurt to try.*

I was just beginning to glimpse the fact that God wanted to be involved in the "dailies" of my life. He is concerned with every circumstance. Every detail.

But I was still unsure of my ground. Somehow I didn't know how I could ask God's help for my little everyday, mundane problems when so many people had such gigantic needs. I guess I thought that God had a priority list on answering prayer. And my needs were so insignificant they were sure to be on the very bottom.

But Psalm 139 was a revelation. To my joy I had discovered in that Scripture that God knows every thought I am thinking. When I sit down. When I stand up. He even knew what my nose and mouth and arms and legs were going to look like . . . before I was conceived. And the psalmist summarizes it all when he says, "How precious also are Thy thoughts to me, O God! How vast is the sum of them! If I should count them, they would outnumber the sand" (139:17). What an overwhelming thought!

How many grains of sand are there in the world? Dividing the days of my life into *that* sum made me aware that He must be thinking millions, even billions of thoughts about me every single day. Therefore nothing was too little to ask Him about. Or too big. He might just be *waiting* for me to ask.

So on that street corner I bowed my head (at this point in my life I still didn't think I could pray with my eyes open) and asked the Lord to help me get to the doctor's office on time.

Jack and I were new to Portland, and I knew only a few people in the city. I'm not sure how I expected God to answer that prayer, but I think I hoped He'd hurry along the next bus which wasn't due for 20 minutes so I could make the proper transfers.

Instead, as I opened my eyes, a car pulled alongside the curb, and a feminine voice asked, "Hi, Carole. Where are you headed?" She was one of that little number of people I knew in all of Portland. When I told her where I was going, she responded, "I'm driving to within a block of there. Hop in."

I was astounded. (Ever pray and then be astonished when God answers? It still happens to me.) I couldn't let it go at that. So I said to my friend, "I suppose you go this way all the time?"

She answered, "No, this is the first time I've gone this way in a year."

My dam of doubt began to show stress. A giant crack appeared. My faith, a mere trickle at first, began to flow more freely. God, the great God of the universe, was personally interested in the tiniest happenings of my life.

I began to understand why God said to "ask . . . ask . . . ask. I want you to ask. I beg you to ask. Please ask." He wants us to ask because He won't violate our wills by forcing things on us that we don't care to request of Him. Yet as our perfect Father, He wants us to let Him fill to overflowing every crevice and corner of our lives. Every facet. Every happening.

When I began to talk to God about the little things in my life, my days took on another dimension, a new excitement. To ask for very specific things and see Him answer in very specific ways was a thrill.

A year later my husband and I had opportunity for our faith to grow and flex its weak muscles in a way we wouldn't have chosen. It was perhaps the most concrete way we could have experienced God's direct provision.

Neither Jack nor I had a great deal of money-sense at that time. When we had money, we spent it and sometimes even if we didn't have it, we spent it.

We had moved from a little three-room apartment, furnished with borrowed furniture, to a large old home. We bought some furniture on credit. About the same time our old car gave out and had to be traded in on a new one, also purchased on monthly installments. It happened so subtly, that without realizing what was happening, we woke up one day to the fact that our salary simply wasn't paying the bills each month. We began to put off one credit payment to meet another and even then we barely made it through each month.

We were convicted by the Scripture which says, "Owe nothing to anyone" (Romans 13:8). God began to show us that our life-style wasn't honoring Him.

Our mess was of our own making. We couldn't blame anyone except ourselves. So we asked forgiveness, and then told God we really wanted to learn through it and to do whatever He wanted. We were beginning to see we needed to ask God and wait for His answer instead of taking matters into our own hands.

We considered selling everything, but realized we could get only a fraction of what we needed and would still be in debt. We prayed about my getting a job till all the bills were paid in full. Lynn was two and a half, old enough for nursery school. But through searching the Word, God indicated very clearly that for this period I was to be a "worker at home" (Titus 2:5). What then?

As we sought God's will, He led us to pay all our bills at the beginning of the month; on installment loans we were to pay *more* than was due if we were able; and we were to *trust Him for everything* the rest of each month. Payday was once a month, on the first, which meant that by the fifth we were usually completely without funds.

This terrified me. I knew verses like "My God shall supply all your needs" (Philippians 4:19), and food is definitely a need. But in the back of my doubting heart, I was afraid God *wouldn't* supply and that the total structure of what we were giving our lives to would collapse. A. W. Tozer has said:

> We can prove our faith by our commital to it, and in no other way. . . Pseudo faith always arranges a way out to serve in case God fails it . . . For true faith it is either God or total collapse . . . .
> The man of pseudo faith will fight for his verbal creed but refuse flatly to allow himself to get into a predicament where his future must depend upon that creed being true. *(The Root of the Righteous)*

"Pseudo faith always arranges a way out." I wondered if I had the faith to put myself out on a limb with God where it would be God's provision or total collapse of my faith.

It is a scary thing to be out on that limb. If God failed to come through for us, it would mean the end of our faith, our lifework, the foundation of our living. Yet, if the Word of God wasn't going to prove true, we were wasting our lives.

We prayed. We covenanted with God that we would tell no one what we were doing. We knew that one phone call would bring help from our parents. A hint might bring money from friends.

For six months we lived not knowing if we would have money for the next meal. And God never failed us. Incredible things happened.

An aunt I had never heard from before or since sent a valentine with $5 enclosed. Jack found a wallet with $60 in it, and, on returning it, was rewarded with $10. The owner was surprised that there was any money left in it at all. One day we actually found bags of groceries on our back porch.

During that time Jack had to have an emergency appendectomy. We had no insurance. The same day the hospital bill came, we received a refund on our income tax that paid it in full. The day the doctor's bill arrived, three different men in the church, not knowing our circumstances, gave enough money to *just* cover the amount.

We developed convictions during those months. One was that if God brought in food for the day, we wouldn't try to make it stretch for three. We remembered that manna was good only for one day. So we would eat the food and pray for the next day's supply.

One afternoon Lynn and I were taking our daily walk, and I did not have one penny to buy her the piece of candy which was her usual treat. She cried all the way home. And mommy's heart cried right along with her. It was the only time that happened, and God gave me an insight into mothers who never have treats to give their children.

One week we were especially tested as we ate pancakes for several days in a row. We did have milk and a giant supply of pancake mix.

For the rest of the time, we ate as we would normally have done, often having groups of young people into our home. Sometimes we felt like the widow feeding Elijah (I Kings 17:10-15), wondering if there would be "oil in the barrel," but we were never short of food to serve.

God did not let that limb break. Each month our faith grew a bit stronger.

I could believe Him now to provide us with the physical needs of life, and more easily for the intangibles as well. After years of reaching for spiritual substance only to find air, I was beginning to close the hands of my life around Reality. But my clasp needed further strengthening.

The Listening Heart/5

Earlier, when Jack and I had lived in the South, we had learned a strange new word. It was "druther." People would say, "I'd druther not." Even without an interpreter, we finally figured out it was a way of saying, "I would rather not."

If I'd had my "druthers," our engagement would not have been two and one half years long. But schooling made our druthers invalid.

We were separated by 300 miles for a year of that period. To fight against loneliness, we promised to write to each other every day. Usually we managed to keep that promise.

However, as a busy worker in the field of Christian Education, I soon discovered that I just didn't have the time to *read* those letters every single day. After giving it some thought, I devised a workable plan. I would stack the letters on my desk in the order in which they arrived. Then on Sunday afternoon, when I had some free time, I would open each letter carefully and read it.

Later, when we were finally married and in the frantic pace of graduate school, we decided that we were spending too much time talking to one another. Minutes would grow into wasted hours as we chatted about every little thing that came to mind. So we agreed to carry around a small pad of paper, and when things occurred that should be talked over, we would jot a memo to ourselves. Then after church on Sunday evenings, we would spend two or three hours talking. Referring to our notes, we would discuss items in order of their priority.

By now, you are probably thinking, *That's weird!*

And you are right!

That wasn't the way it happened at all. It is true that we were separated, and that we wrote every day. Our schedules *were* busy. But from there the story differs. I would *run* home during my lunch hour to get those letters! I would read them. Re-read them. And then re-re-read them! When I got home in the evening and had more time, I would read them again, letting them soak in and trying to read between the lines.

After we were married, we really *were* busy with graduate school, jobs and extra activities. But we *talked* —about every little thing and all the big ones too. The greatest complaint in marriages today is the lack of communication, and if we really had done what I first told you, we probably would be divorced by now.

Lovers do not communicate through notebooks. Nor do they stack up love letters to read "when they have time."

During those initial touches of God on my life in Portland, I began to realize that I had in my hands God's great love letter to me—the Bible. Yet I was reading it out of duty, a sort of "If-I-read-a-chapter-God-will-bless-my-day" philosophy. It was not surprising that I seldom experienced *wonder* as I read it. I had been meeting a *habit* rather than meeting God.

As I began to see the Bible as God's personal, intimate letter to me, I found I didn't want to read it only occasionally or just in public, any more than I would read Jack's letters only once a week or in church. I wanted to savour God's Word alone and in quiet.

When a problem arose, I would think, *I must pray about that later,* as if to pull out that little notebook and jot something down to discuss at a later date. I still catch myself doing that on occasion.

But God is *always* present, always listening, always ready to converse. Communication with Him is never broken because *He* doesn't have the time.

Discovering this truth made a permanent difference in my walk with God. Someone once said to me, "I used to read a book, but now I *listen to a voice."* The Bible isn't just another good book. It is a unique message directed to my heart.

I began listening to that Voice—with intensity. Psalm 119:18 became the daily prayer of my time with God. Each day I would begin, "Lord, please give me a W.T. today," which in short-cut language means "Wondrous Thing." That verse prays, "Open Thou mine eyes, that I may behold *wondrous things* out of Thy law" (KJV).

Every morning I vowed not to stop reading till God had given me that wondrous thing from His Word. And He always did. Sometimes when I got bogged down in Leviticus, I'd have to read as many as five chapters, but the Lord always gave a fresh taste from His banquet of wondrous things.

Later, I found I didn't need to *get* something from the Lord. It was enough just to enjoy His presence and fellowship. However, in these early days, I needed that special "W.T.," and God made sure it was mine.

I didn't start big. A few minutes of *quality* time became my objective. For me, five minutes of real heart communication with my husband was valued more than two hours in front of the T.V. So I prayed for quality time with God rather than quantity. Seven minutes is about the time it takes for me to shower, dress or make up my face. I was sure there were at least seven minutes that I could spare to spend with the One who loved me most of all.

Those brief moments were spent something like this:

The first half minute I prayed for God to open my eyes to the truth He had for me that day. Many times I just prayed Psalm 119:18 again, for my heart to be opened to all those wonderful things from His Word.

The next four minutes I read a portion from His love letter. It took me weeks to read Mark, then John, then on to Paul's letters to young churches. I didn't try to get through an entire chapter in those minutes. Sometimes it was a paragraph, sometimes just a few verses. I would think about it, pray concerning it and underline those verses that had significant meaning to me.

My reading was followed by about two and a half minutes of conversing with God, talking to Him about my own needs and those of my family and friends. There were times of confession when God reproved me of wrongs I had done. Times of thanksgiving. Times of praise.*

My seven minutes became 10, then 15, and eventually even longer. There didn't seem to be time enough to talk with God about all He was doing in my life.

At first, I tried to have this time before my first cup of coffee. I had heard such maxims as, "No Bible, no breakfast," and, "Talk to God about men before you talk to

---

*This practical devotional plan has been published in a helpful pamphlet, *Seven Minutes with God,* and is available from your local bookstore.

men about God." This last one I mentally condensed to: "Talk to God before you talk to others." But I found my mind to be a fog of disconnected thoughts before breakfast.

And God deserves the *best* part of my day. Generally, for me, the best time has been after breakfast when my husband has left for work and before the activities of the day press in. So that was when I determined to meet with God. But some of my days were so full that there wasn't a minute to spare after breakfast. At those times, I asked God for His strength to get up a bit earlier, to erase the drowsy fog from my mind and keep me alert to spend a few moments with Him *before* breakfast.

I have a friend whose small children get up the minute they hear a sound from her. So the best part of her day is when her three take naps. Before getting out of bed, she takes a minute to turn the day over to the Lord and to say good morning to Him. She asks Him to draw her thoughts to Him through the day. Then when the kids go down for naps, she takes a few minutes for her special time with God.

Another friend is most alert about midnight. He spends the last hour of the day, the best part of *his* day, with God.

Probably for most of us, the earlier we can do this, the better it will be. God desires *our* presence. "True worshipers shall worship the Father in spirit and truth; for such people the Father *seeks* to be His worshipers" (John 4:23). Isn't that something? And because He desires to have fellowship with *us,* He will help us and give us strength to meet with Him. He won't violate our wills by *making* us spend time with Him. But He is able to even "make us willing" if we ask Him to give us the desire for this fellowship with Him.

This is one thing about which we can't be haphazard. It takes *conviction* in our hearts. The conviction must be that spending time with God is not just beneficial, but essential— essential for our very breath as Christians, for our lives, for

our growth. It means *determining to do this without fail.*
I was determined.

He was talking; I was listening.

But I needed to know how to take what He was telling me and make it workable in my daily life.

The Applying Heart/6

I was painting a chair in the kitchen one morning and had stopped for a minute to put on the coffee, leaving an open can of paint sitting on a rag on the kitchen counter.

As I turned my back, our little daughter toddled over and gave the rag a big yank. The almost-full can of paint toppled over onto Lynn, the chair, the floor and a little bit on me as I rushed, too late, to stop the disaster.

All I could do was stand there in consternation saying over and over, "Oh, Lynn . . . ooooooh Lynn. O *Lynn!*"

An hour later, with the mess cleaned up the best I could, I went upstairs congratulating myself that I hadn't lost my temper and spanked Lynn. I knew she felt bad and hadn't really meant to do anything naughty, but my temper sometimes flares quickly in a situation like that.

In stretching to pat myself on the back, I almost missed hearing the still small Voice. "Carole," God seemed to be saying, "you have just memorized the verse. Now learn it by heart. 'In *everything* give thanks, for this is the will of God in

Christ Jesus concerning you'" (I Thessalonians 5:18, KJV).

I was shocked. I answered, "Now, Lord, You don't mean that I am to give thanks for spilled paint and messes in kitchens? You couldn't mean *that."*

The answer came: "In *everything."*

God meant it. And meaning it, He not only showed me *how* to do it, but gave me the ability.

I couldn't figure out the "why" right then of giving thanks for spilled paint. And I am a "why" person. Later on, God began to show me some of the reasons for having a thankful spirit whether or not I can understand the reason for the event itself. At that moment, however, He was just telling me to be thankful without the understanding. I had held my temper, true. But in no way was I *thankful.*

So I stopped and said, "All right, Lord. I don't understand it all, but thank You. Thank You for the spilled paint and the job I had cleaning it up too."

The Son broke through. A spirit of thankfulness cannot coexist with a grumbling heart.

Paul's exhortation to constant thankfulness was not a new concept to me. I had read it a hundred times. And each time I read it I would throw up my mental hands in frustration and despair and think, *That is humanly impossible.*

But just before the incident of the spilled paint, a tool was offered me which helped me take this command out of the impossible category and make it workable.

I was already learning to study the Bible while having a conversation with God, asking Him to say to me clearly, "Take special note. This is for you today." When He speaks in this way, we need to underline the verse or write it down on paper.

Now I was discovering how He uses the everyday events to *emphasize* these lessons.

Later, I wrote down an application using the tool which

had been suggested as a part of a Navigator weekly Bible study.

Mine went like this:

1. *Write the verse in your own words.* As you have prayed and God has emphasized a portion of His Word to your heart, underline it or write it in a notebook. Now take the verse and write it out the way you would express it.

I wrote on I Thessalonians 5:18: "Paul says I am to give thanks no matter what happens, because it is God's will for my life when I am in Christ."

2. *Write out how you have failed to obey the verse.* Use personal pronouns—*I* and *me,* not *we* and *us.*

That wasn't hard. I wrote, "I just don't give thanks in a whole lot of things—things I can't understand, things I don't like, things that are hard!"

3. *Give a specific example of how you have failed to obey this verse.*

That wasn't hard either, as God had just given me a graphic experience with the spilled paint! I wrote, "When Lynn spilled the paint all over my kitchen floor this week, I certainly didn't give thanks."

4. *Pray for God's guidance. Then think of a practical plan to put the verse into your life.* Two guidelines are helpful here: (1) The plan should be one that can be done within one week's time or you will be working on several at one time. (2) If possible, have someone check you at the end of the week to see if you have accomplished your goal.

That was the most difficult. Finally, God showed me that one of my problems was a time of a most intense DRA, which, in our household, stands for "Dirty Rotten Attitude." For me it was just before supper.

We were now working with The Navigators and had a large old home with several people living with us. We have found over the years that a living situation can be used of God to train men and women in various aspects of character and ministry. In His training program, however, it is usually the ones in charge who actually receive the most help.

Because of the work schedules of the men living in our home, dinner had to be at 6 P.M. sharp. And punctuality isn't one of my strong points.

One of the men would come in about 5:45 P.M. and start to tease Lynn. She was tired and a bit cranky about then, and this teasing would end up with her in tears, hanging on to my skirt. Result: dinner impeded, clenched teeth, DRA.

But we have a creative God. Ideas from Him began to formulate. So my plan went something like this:

"During this next week I will: (1) Pray at least three times during the day to have the spirit of thankfulness. (2) Ask those in the home to pray this with me. (3) Talk to the man who was teasing Lynn and suggest he take her out to swing or play hide-n-seek for that 15 minutes before dinner. (I knew he wasn't teasing her for meanness. He wanted to be friends with her, but didn't know how.) (4) Sit down for a 10-minute break about 4 P.M. to pull myself together, pray and have a brief moment with Lynn before the pressure begins."

And I did it. I found that instead of getting frantic, I was actually giving thanks.

The key to unlocking the practical door of personal application is the *plan of action.* Some commands are easier to make concrete than others, so ask God to speak to you about this kind first.

One example would be the command to "love your neighbor as yourself." Not many of us really do that. In applying this verse one week, my second point of the outline stated, "I just *don't* love people like I do myself."

But the third and fourth points of the outline are critical. So I wrote, "I especially have problems with my obnoxious neighbor who complains every time my child runs across her lawn."

Now how can you love someone you don't *like?* The enemy of our souls just doesn't want us to get that practical. Satan will block us here if he can.

As I prayed, ideas emerged. I wrote: (1) I will memorize two verses on love besides 'Love your neighbor as yourself.' (2) I will bake some cookies to take to my neighbor. (3) I will invite her to lunch this week and try to find out what is making her so unhappy. (4) I will pray for her every day asking God to help her and use me as a channel of His love for her. Also to *like* her."

And it worked.

Try this personal application outline every week in connection with your Bible reading or preferably with a weekly Bible study program.

Satan will fight you.

But God will help you.

And God is bigger.

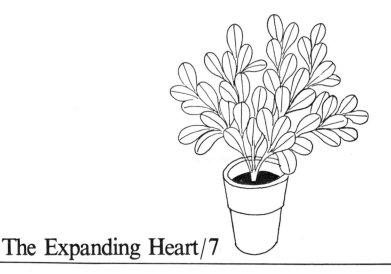

The Expanding Heart/7

I was seven years old and I was lost.

A move to a new town was complicated by my brother catching a virus. Usually we went to church as a family, but this Sunday morning Daddy drove me to a new Sunday School three blocks away and went back to help Mom with my sick brother. Daddy gave me directions to walk home. Two blocks north and one block west.

I went two blocks west and one block north and found myself totally disoriented—and scared.

Unsuccessfully choking back sobs, I prayed, "Lord, please find me."

My relief was great as I opened my eyes to see Daddy's car coming toward me down the street. "Before they call, I will answer" (Isaiah 65:24) wasn't a promise I knew at that age, but God was fulfilling it for me.

That was the first specific answer to prayer I remember.

Some things I learn slowly, and in others I am a downright turtle. In learning some aspects of prayer, I generally fall into the latter category. Fortunately, God is a patient teacher.

I enrolled in the kindergarten of the school of prayer as an adult and my first primer contained blank pages. I was soon to learn the purpose of those pages. It came under the title of "How to Get Organized." Organized I was not.

Living on a "miracle plane" isn't achieved in a day. Grudgingly at first, I began to write on those blank pages.

First, I wrote down everything I felt a need to pray about—current needs, people, friends whom I had promised to pray for (and sometimes forgot to remember), our nation, our church. The list looked horrendous! I am glad there was a second step.

I then divided this list into two separate pages of requests. One page was for current and immediate needs that required specific answers within a certain period of time—people who were ill, a financial crisis, a desperate situation. I wrote these requests on the left side of the paper, put a line down the middle and dated the request. On the right side at the top, I wrote "Answers."

The second list was for people for whom I wanted to pray, but didn't know of any urgent or special request—family, friends, the church, missionaries, countries. I grouped these and put an equal number of items under each of the six days of the week, leaving Sunday free.

Later, I added a page of requests for my husband and one page for my daughter.

I began with a rather doubtful attitude. But soon my skepticism was eroded as my "answer" side began to fill so that I had to begin a fresh page.

God always answers. As with a human parent, there are times when that answer has to be "no," and a very firm "no" at that. At other times God says, "Wait awhile. The time is not right." I learned to record these as well. In retrospect, I have sometimes thanked Him more for the "no" answers than the "yes" ones, as I have seen His wisdom in delivering me from some things I thought were "musts."

Before, when I had to wait a long time for an answer that was especially important, I tended to think, *Well, God isn't answering my prayers anymore.* Then I wondered if He ever had. (Sometimes my memory gets rather short!)

With that list before me, I discovered I couldn't doubt God was meeting my needs in exciting ways even when those "wait" or "no" answers appeared frequently on my list.

One day it occurred to me that if I spent just a fraction of the time praying for my husband that I spent in washing, ironing and cooking for him, the investment might bring dividends in great proportion. My application for that week was to spend 10 minutes a day praying just for *Jack.* I didn't think 10 minutes would bankrupt my day.

I looked at my watch as I began. I prayed and prayed. When I glanced at my watch again, one minute had elapsed.

I started again and found myself praying for the people he was meeting, his work and various other things. But my covenant had been to pray for *Jack,* not things related to him.

Finally, I had to pray to learn how to pray. And God answered. That very day I found I was praying about things I had never thought to *think* about, let alone pray about. I didn't tell my husband what I was doing, but he began asking me to pray things for him that he had never mentioned before.

Most of us spend considerable hours thinking about the advice we'd like to give our husbands. Some of us give it. What greater things would be accomplished in their lives if we would spend at least an equal time in prayer for them.

It took only a few months to convince me of the value of writing down my prayer requests. When the enemy would tempt me to think that something was mere coincidence, all I had to do was look over page upon page of specific answers, and Satan had to close his mouth.

God is not only the God of the dailies, He is God of the delights. David says, "The Lord be magnified, who delights in the prosperity of His servant" (Psalm 35:27). God *delights* to delight us.

If "prayer is the conversation between two people who love each other," then talking with God about needs, wants and even wishes is something He wants us to do. If we just talk to Him about our *needs,* that leaves Him out of vast areas of our lives. And I am convinced He wants to be included in everything. He wants to be asked about everything. We know from the Bible that God is the giver of *all* good things, but if we don't ask, how are we going to know that it is God who is pouring forth His love in giving us great and wonderful things?

I was ready to proceed to First Grade. So I began what I call my "blessing list."

Throughout the day I would ask for little things, and God would answer. Sometimes I wouldn't have time to even say "Thank you." Most of those things would be forgotten the next day. Keeping a little diary and writing down those blessings from God is an experience that would charge up the driest battery. One week I wrote 121 items on my "blessing list." These were specific answers during the day such as parking places, finding things that are lost, patience with a trying phone call.

In the last few years of the school of prayer, God has excited me with what I call my "bonus list." Remember, God delights to delight us. So this is a list that I keep just to talk to the Lord about the "It-sure-would-be-nice-to-have-things."

James tells us that "you do not have because you do not ask" (James 4:2). He goes on to say that "you ask and do not receive, because you ask with wrong motives, so that you may spend it on your pleasures" (4:3). I take that to mean that God knows it wouldn't be good for me to have some things that might contribute to my selfishness and thus become sin. Therefore the things on my bonus list are those for which I am careful to say, "If it wouldn't be good for me to have, Lord, I don't want it. But if it would delight Your heart to delight *my* heart in this way, I would be most grateful."

My love for God has grown in realizing how graciously He gives me the "desires of my heart." He isn't a grudging giver. He *wants* to thrill my heart with His goodness.

I have big things, little things, silly and not-so-silly things on my bonus list.

One summer we traveled to the West Coast and into Canada. We found some of the most beautiful scenery in the world driving the 60 miles from Banff to Jasper National Park. All three of us were enjoying the magnificent views. But 10-year-old Lynn and I especially wanted to see some wild animals.

Now we didn't *need* to see wild animals. We just *wanted to see them.*

We decided to ask God about this.

You would not believe the wild animals we saw. It took us all day to travel that 60 miles because we had to stop, get out and take pictures at every bend in the road. We saw bear, deer, elk, moose, and mountain goats. There was even a deer and her fawn walking down main street in the town of Jasper.

The next day on the ride back I thought, *I wonder if people just naturally see a lot of wild animals up here in the summer? Could it be a coincidence?* (You can see I still needed a lot of growing in faith.) So we didn't pray to see any animals on the way back, *and we didn't see one.*

I have prayed for big things such as the opportunity to travel overseas. Two years after this was put on my bonus list, we were on our way around the world. The trip was one of expanding my horizons and deepening my concern for missionaries and nations. The money for the trip was provided in such a way that I had no doubt it was from a God who delights to *give* to His children.

I have prayed for landscaping and shoes and new coats. A coat when you don't have one is a *need* and can be put on your specific prayer list. Many times I have prayed for a coat as a definite *need.*

One winter a few years ago I found myself with a threadbare, but serviceable coat. I didn't really like that coat, but I couldn't honestly say I needed a new one. So I put a new coat on the "bonus" page and asked God that if it would please Him, I would surely appreciate another coat.

Within four days I was given *three* coats. I had the fun of giving two away to friends who were more in need than I was. That was a bonus on the bonus.

I received a letter once from a woman who had heard me talk about bonus praying. She wrote:

> I think that I like many others sort of *wish* this or that in the line of a bonus prayer idea, but never really put them down and really expect an answer. Like I needed, I thought, good weather this year for one of my car pools. The roads to this one school are really impossible, and I thought this a good bonus prayer. Would you believe that God outdid Himself, and provided a bus service that we found out we should have had seven years ago? Such an answer and blessing was beyond anything I could think of, and all I asked for was a little good weather.
>
> . . . one rather new Christian gal in my Bible study really was challenged, as her prayer life was not too great. Her daily prayers began to be answered, and then she tried the bonus idea, for her husband's promotion, as it seemed impossible (he is in the service). After a week, nothing. And she said, "I

just told the Lord I have to have this answer on my Bonus
Prayer List, please show me You hear me" . . . Within hours
her husband's promotion came through, and he was shocked.

All she would say over and over was, "I knew it would
happen today."

Actually, that *isn't* the kind of thing one should ask for in
that way. A bonus prayer should never be demanded nor
should we think that it is something that is our right.

But isn't it beautiful the way the Lord honored this new
Christian and helped her faith grow by giving her this bonus?
In her book *By Searching,* Isobel Kuhn tells of the incredible
things God did for her to prove Himself even before she
became a Christian. Many times we pray "all wrong," but
with God it is "all right."

A current lesson I am exploring is how to *listen* in prayer.
Most of the time we talk so loud and fast that we don't give
God a chance to say anything.

The first time I began to get a glimmer of how God speaks
so directly to my heart if I will listen was in a crisis situation.

It had been one of *those* months. My world had fallen in
on top of me and all I could do was lie amidst the rubble.
Two very precious friends were in the hospital with
emotional illnesses; the troubled waters of other friends and
relatives were deep and dark and heavy; a flood in our lower
level had left us with much repairing and redecoration to do,
causing the whole house to be torn up for two months.

Then one afternoon my husband told me that an
emotionally distraught young man was coming over. He
wanted the household to be quiet as he talked with this
person in the living room. That meant I had to sit by the
phone to grab it on the first ring.

I went down into our rugless, messy bedroom and
collapsed on the cement floor by the bed (right beside the
telephone) and buried my face in my hands.

There I cried and sobbed and prayed. Several years

before, I had memorized Psalm 62:8, which says, "Trust in [the Lord] at all times, O people; pour out your heart before Him; God is a refuge for us." In my most depressed and anxious moments, I would go to God and tell Him *all* about it—every little detail, every complaint, every heartache, every frustration. I literally "poured out my heart" to Him.

What a comfort it is to take all to the God who listens with compassion and can be trusted not only to be compassionate, but who is able to *do* something about it.

That day I told Him all my problems beginning with A and going on way past Z. Then I said, "Lord, I've had it! I've had it up to here. I just can't take any more. I feel like going away, running off and hiding."

Then I waited.

Waited for Him to answer back.

I fully expected Him in the quietness of my own heart to tell me what He often tells me through His Word, to "give thanks in everything." But He didn't do that.

Or, I thought maybe He would tell me to count my blessings, because I really had a great many even though I wasn't appreciating them at that moment. But He didn't tell me that either.

Instead, very quietly but distinctly, God impressed on my heart two words, "Go ahead."

I said audibly, "I beg Your pardon, Lord?" I thought I must be putting words into my own mind because somehow that answer didn't make any sense to me.

But again, the firm directive came, "Go ahead and hide. Hide . . . in Me."

Suddenly all the verses in the Psalms about God being the "cleft of the rock in which to hide" rushed into my memory. I had never thought about what that really meant . . . to *hide* in God.

Quickly I began looking up the verses in a Bible

concordance that mention God as our "hiding place."

And what a joy that was. All my frustrations and cares were swept up and discarded as God picked me up from the rubble of self-pity and hid me in the Rock of Ages.

The house didn't get cleaned up the next week. And the people I was so concerned about didn't suddenly get well. In fact, all the problems I had been having were still right there with me.

But throughout the whole week I went around "hiding" in God. I thought, *You may see me, but you can't touch me, because I'm hiding this week,* and I really was. Interestingly enough, nothing touched the "inner me" all that week. And I learned a little about what it meant that God was literally a "shelter, a cleft, a hiding place" for our weary hearts and souls.

The next week the impression came: "OK, Carole, you've been hiding long enough. Time for you to come fight in the battle now." By then I was strengthened and refreshed to do just that.

So often I don't take the time I need to just *listen* to God after I have talked to Him. Yet conversation is two-way or it isn't conversation at all. And prayer is really conversing with God. Prayer is not only our speaking to Him, but also listening to what God may want to say to us through His Word and the concepts that are taught in His Word. This "listening" to Him in prayer is still comparatively new to me, and I am excited about the possibilities that are ahead.

Jeremiah said, "The Lord's lovingkindnesses indeed never cease, for His compassions never fail. They are new every morning" (Lamentations 3:22, 23).

New every morning. What new thing is He doing for you today? For me? During a whole period in my life, I asked that God specifically show me one *new* thing He was pointing out to me each week about Himself, and He faithfully did just that—an aspect of His holiness, of His personal love, of His greatness. He is a many-splendored God. Yet we experience so little of Him because we don't *ask*.

"Ask," Jesus stated, "and you will receive, that your joy may be made full" (John 16:24).

Interlude: Poems of Prayer

Recently, I have been writing out prayers as God has brought them to my mind while reading His Word. Here are a few of them.

There's so much of me in me, Lord.

I ask
that as I get older
You won't let all the *me* in me
Solidify.
So that You can't
empty me
of
myself.

So that I can't be filled with You.
So that I'm not pliable
usable
moldable
shapable.

Because most of all, Lord
I desire to be
molded by Your hand
filled by Your Spirit
used for Your service.

That takes emptying—of me.

And filling full with *You.*

Help me, Lord.

Lord,
>How glad I am
>that I never have
>to get lonesome for You.

Because You never leave!

Thank You, Lord.

My daughter is getting married.
She's left our home
To establish her own.

And that's right, Lord.

But sometimes I get so lonely for her.
>her bright smile
>her women-talk
>her sensitive understanding
>>and insight.

My sweetheart is away on a trip
Impossible for me to go this time.
I miss him achingly.
With my whole being.

And that's right too, Lord.

But how thrilled I am
That I never have
To get lonesome for You.

Thank You.

From Ephesians 3:16-19

Lord,
   I'm beginning to see
   That it's not what I know
         about You
   But knowing You.

   Not how to work with people
   But looking into Your face.

   Not the principles of group discussion
         or even how to explain the Good News.

   But knowing the
               height
               breadth
               length
               depth
   of the love of Christ.

   Oh, God.
         Help me to *know You.*

From Colossians 3:1-11

Lord,
    my mind gets so absorbed
    in mundane, routine, nothing things;
    in cares
    hurts
    problems that persist
    petty annoyances.

There are good things too:
    my daughter's wedding plans
    cooking to entertain Your children
    making a haven for my husband.

But You've said,
        "Set your mind on things above."

I guess that really means
        staying my thoughts on You
        reflecting on eternal things
        keeping Heaven more alive in my
            heart than my earthly home.

My momentary thoughts are of heaven.

My major interests are here.

That needs to be reversed.
    Help me.

From I John 4:18

Dear Lord,
   You've just said to me that worry
      is a type of fear.
   And You said that "perfect love casts
      out fear."
   Perfect, mature love won't be afraid.

   If I really love You in an adult way
   My trust of You is
      full
      complete.

   I wouldn't worry . . .

   When Lynn is driving in a storm
   When the way of life is foggy
      and seems so muddled
   When I get put down
   When Jack feels he's made an
      irreparable blunder.
   when I have too much to do
      and too little time to do it.
   When I'm helpless
         tired
         frustrated.

Worry is fear.

> You are strong.
> You go before.
> You care.
>
> Why do I worry?

Help me, Lord.

From James 3

Oh God,
    I hurt.

I just saw me in all my wretchedness.

Buried under all my pious do-goody things
way down there where my own heart
        was totally unaware
lies an awful heap of dirt.

You've uncovered it.

It hurts.
I hurt.

I've been praying against selfish ambition
        and bitter jealousy
        for others.

Now I see it in me.
        subtle
        indistinct
        but there.

Cleanse it out, Lord.

From Revelation 5

Oh Lord, You are *Worthy!*

Today I read in Your Book
That there wasn't found anywhere
      on the earth
      in Heaven
      under the earth

Anyone
      no man
      nor angel
worthy.

No one could open THE BOOK
      that Book of Life
Because no one had given Life.

Then You stepped forward.
In the form of a Lamb slain
And You opened the Book!

You are *worthy,* Lord.

Because You redeemed men from every
      tribe
      tongue
      people
      nation.

You redeemed me.

Thank You.

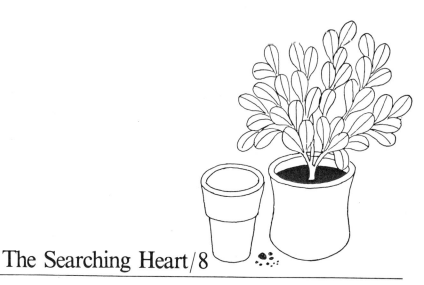

The Searching Heart/8

The first things I hung up in our new home in Colorado were three little flowered wall tiles with one word on each. "Faith," "Hope" and "Love" were placed with loving care in our guest bathroom.

Soon after we moved, the dry climate loosened one, causing it to fall and smash beyond repair. A member of the family had forgotten to tell me that it had been swept up and discarded.

In housecleaning later, I discovered the tile missing. I thought, *How awful. "Hope" is gone!*

I hadn't thought much about *hope* in recent days. But how terrible if we have no hope. Not the "I-hope-so" kind of hope, of course. But the sure hope that Scripture talks about, personified in Jesus. The Bible tells us that Christ *is* our hope. It is only through our sure Hope that we can *know* we have all the things He has promised. Many promises are for the here and now. And many more for the future.

I looked up some of these verses about hope the next

week. They were such a delight that I laughed aloud alone in the bedroom. And suddenly I was again reminded of the *joy* of the Word of God. David said it was his *delight* (Psalm 119:24). It can be a delight from the start of a Christian life, but it took years for it to be that for me.

A lovely woman once asked a group of us, "If your husband were asked to name a woman he considered to be 'godly,' whom would he name?"

My first thought was, *Well, it certainly wouldn't be me!*

My second thought answered back, *True! But why not?*

It was then I discovered a passage of Scripture that lets us in on the "secret of godliness"—II Peter 1:3-8.

Peter says that through God's divine power, we have been given "everything pertaining to life and godliness" (verse 3). The moment we have Christ we have everything we need to be godly, really godly. Nothing has to be grafted on or grown later.

Then he adds "through the true knowledge of Him [Christ]." The secret of being godly comes in *knowing,* really knowing, Christ. And the secret of knowing Christ comes in knowing the Word, the "precious promises" of verse four.

He continues and tells us how we are to obtain and learn about these promises (verses 5-8). And diligence is the key. Diligence and discipline.

We don't like those words, or at least I don't. But if a million dollars in gold were buried in your backyard, wouldn't you be foolish to leave it there? It might take some diligence for you to dig it up, but you would certainly find the time to do it. Otherwise you could be a rich person, yet starve to death.

We can "dig up" the spiritual riches we have in God's Word in five basic ways.

- We *hear* it—in church, Sunday School, on the radio
- We *read* it

- We *study* it
- We *memorize* it
- We *meditate* on it

Most of us hear the Word a great deal, read it some, rarely study it, never memorize it and meditate on it only by chance rather than design.

If we put these methods of intake into the form of a hand in which to grasp the Word, it should look like this:

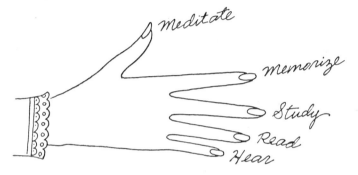

In the beginning, my spiritual intake "hand" was very strange looking. It looked something like this:

I wasn't studying consistently, memorizing at all and I

certainly didn't know how to go about meditating on the Word, so I rarely applied what I *did* know. In a previous chapter I've told about how I began to memorize and meditate. In due course of time I learned a simple form of Bible study which helped me begin digging out some of God's treasures.

I needed something simple. The more complex ways of study which I had learned were of value to me, when I had the energy to do them. But they couldn't be used to help the high schoolers we were working with who were coming to Christ. And, after a spurt of energy, my own Bible study would diminish and it might be months before I'd have another surge.

I discovered I wasn't alone.

My husband had asked a group of 40 Christian Sunday School and church workers in an anonymous quiz how many were doing consistent Bible study and what kind.

I compiled the answers the next evening, and they were sadly revealing.

Apart from studying their Sunday School lessons in order to teach their classes, only seven out of the 40 did regular Bible study. Of the seven, four considered reading a daily devotional book their Bible study and one listened to a Christian broadcasting station. Only two of the seven had a plan to do original, systematic Bible study each week for their own personal growth.

I was ready for the plan that was shown me. It was a plan from The Navigators, and it was so simple that it could be used with either a verse of Scripture, a paragraph or a chapter. At first the mechanics of doing even this uncomplicated form stopped me from fully enjoying Bible study. But because it *was* simple, I found the joy of discovery before I had time to get discouraged at the digging process. The plan was also easy to explain and would help new

Christians or those who didn't yet know Christ, but who wanted to study the Bible.

The study consists of four steps:

1. *What does it say?* Half of my problems came from not knowing what the Bible was saying—*really* saying, that is. So I began to write the Scripture out in my own words, paraphrasing it, reading it in context, looking up other translations of the verse or passage till I truly felt I knew what it was saying.

2. *What does it say that I don't understand?* I learned to ask questions about the passage which caused me to search the Bible. At first my questions were superficial and were problems that were easily answered by other verses or by the context itself. Later I saw the value of asking questions that were more searching, requiring greater study. Depth questions. Many that could not be answered easily. I found that one can never exhaust the depths and meaning of the Bible.

I also discovered that I did not always have to find answers for my questions, but that the actual *thinking up* of things I did not understand was part of this study. Often, answers came much later, sometimes in subsequent studies.

3. *What does it say elsewhere in the Scriptures?* Someone told me that the Bible is its own best commentary. So I learned not only to find other Scripture that would add something to the verse I was studying, but would also answer the questions I had just asked. I began to do mini-topical studies from my questions and to research wonderful truths in this way. Yet for a new Christian, one other verse often is all that she needs to thrill her with the sense of discovery.

4. *What does it say to me?* This is the hardest, yet most important. This is the personal application aspect which was discussed in an earlier chapter. Each verse or passage can be used of God to speak directly to us. I needed a tool to take passages from pleasant-but-plastic-theory to patent-leather reality, and God showed me what to do.

These four study questions are as simple or as deep as you want to go. Something you can do in 10 minutes or 10 hours. They are pass-on-able, practical, and precious to a growing Christian.

Try it this week with just two verses, Proverbs 3:5, 6: "Trust in the Lord with all your heart, and do not lean on your own understanding. In all your ways acknowledge Him, and He will make your paths straight."

Next week take a paragraph, like the first major paragraph of Philippians 4 (verses 1-9). The following week you might want to try a whole chapter, such as the third chapter of James.

The story is told of a young woman who was given a book which, as she tried to read it, she found dull and uninteresting. She put it aside after reading only a few chapters.

A few months later she went on a cruise and met and fell in love with a young man. One day she said to him, "You know, I have a book in my library written by a man with a name just like yours."

"What's the name of the book?" he inquired.

When she told him, he said, "That's not so strange. I wrote that book."

Fortunately, he didn't ask her what she thought of it.

When she returned home, she immediately located the book, dusted it off and read it from cover to cover.

And she found it to be the most fascinating book she'd ever read.

What made the difference? She had met and fallen in love with the author.

When we meet Christ and fall in love with Him, the Bible takes on an entirely new meaning for us. He is the Author, and He says, "Every word of God *proves* true" (Proverbs 30:5, LB). When we find it difficult to understand, the Author Himself explains His Book to us. And as the Spirit of Christ gives us light concerning its contents, we will fall even *more* in love with Him.

I was beginning to find treasure. And it thrilled me. Today I feel like I've just opened the door a crack to the stores in God's treasure house. I can hardly wait to find out what else is inside.

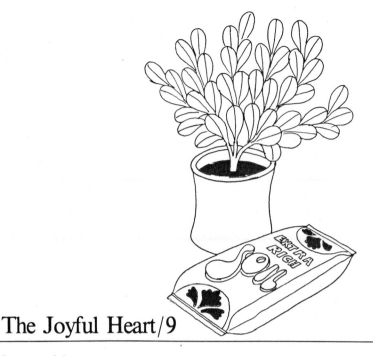

The Joyful Heart/9

It was a Monday. I looked at the day. It glared back at me. And the day was just too big for me.

There was nothing particularly wrong with that Monday. But there was nothing right about it either. Jack had been gone for a week, and wasn't due to return for another week. The weather was dark and rainy. Nothing loomed to brighten my horizon. A little black cloud hung over my head.

That day is vivid to me because on that day I learned something about the *joy* of the Christian life. When a difficult day comes, Christians are to "consider it joy" (James 1:2). But how in the world do I *do that?*

My own definition of "grace"—which some briefly define as "unmerited favor"—is "whatever I need whenever I need it." It may not be the most theological definition, but after studying many Bible verses on "grace," that is my conclusion.

And on that gloomy Monday, what did I need? Well, I

didn't need strength to lead a Bible study or wisdom to counsel a friend. I was stuck at home without a car, and the day looked like one blah day in my economy. I just needed the "bubble of joy" in my heart to be able to *feel* the truth of the verse, "This is the day which the Lord has made; let us rejoice and be glad in it" (Psalm 118:24).

There is no switch to flip to get instant "rejoice." No crank to turn for gladness. No pump to prime for joy.

I needed God's *grace.*

So I prayed, "Lord, what I need today is Your grace to give me joy, a fruit of the Spirit. I ask You for a happy heart."

And He answered. It was an exciting day. Not because anything special happened, but because He made the everyday things *special in themselves.*

A little poem goes:

> Life is a trial mile by mile.
> Life is hard, yard by yard.
> But it's a cinch, inch by inch.

Taking each "inch" of life with God in full control makes life joyous. Our hearts should always have that little bubble of joy simmering away on the back burner. It is just a little "blip . . . blip . . . blip" as the joy bubbles like a simmering teapot, exploding occasionally into a full boil. But if there isn't any "blip" of joy at all in our hearts, then we know something is wrong in our relationship with the Source of all joy, God Himself. Joy is a fruit of the Holy Spirit (Galatians 5:22, 23), and we have every right to expect it as a part of our lives with Him.

Scripture versions use the words interchangeably, but I differentiate "joy" from "happiness." To me, happiness depends a great deal on circumstances. I am not happy about surgery, illness, tragedy or death. But my *joy* should always be there; it should remain constant.

If God is the source of real joy, then the depth of our enjoyment in the Christian life is directly related to *understanding* and *knowing* Him. A paraphrased translation reads, "Base your *happiness* on your hope in Christ" (Romans 12:12, PH). The psalmist says about God, "You have endowed him [man] with eternal happiness. You have given him the unquenchable *joy* of Your presence" (Psalm 21:6, LB).

Amazing! Consider these words of the psalmist, "He is my strength, my shield from every danger. I trusted in Him, and He helped me! *Joy* rises in my heart until I burst out in songs of praise to Him" (Psalm 28:7, LB).

I seem to know this in my *head,* but sometimes it takes awhile to creep the 13 inches to my *heart.*

So I pondered, *How is it possible to have consistent joy? It is God's grace that gives joy, but how do I have it as a continuous part of my life?*

I concluded there were several ingredients that, when blended together, insure a "bubble of joy" in my life.

The first of these is "living on a miracle plane" in prayer. That means seeing God in the dailies, in the bonuses, in the blessings and in the wants as well as the needs. Jesus tells me that I am to *"ask* that my *joy* may be made full" (John 16:24). Fullness of joy depends a great deal on how much I am seeing God through answered prayer.

Joy also depends on how clearly I am seeing God through His Word. God has written "these things"—His words—so that I might have *joy* (John 15:11).

Here it is again. I can't get away from it. The depth of my joy depends on how deeply I am being rooted in the rich soil of God's Word.

Another facet of joy is reflected by my knowing and *accepting* God's immense love for me—personally.

In Forest Lawn Cemetery in California stands a lifelike statue of a little girl, a small boy and a tiny dog looking up to a wall on which the Founder's Creed is carved. Part of this creed says, "Most of all I believe in a Christ who smiles and loves you and me."

But do I? Do I *really?* In my early years I often thought of God as frowning at me. Now I know that He smiles at me. I am beginning to understand the truth Paul was trying to impress on us, "He has showered down upon us the richness of His grace—for how well He understands us and knows what is best for us at all times" (Ephesians 1:8, LB).

If we could only fathom a part of the magnitude of His love for us—if we could grasp it with our total beings—that bubble of joy would erupt so violently that it would explode into the darkest corners of our lives.

One of the areas flushed clean would be the one in which we have hidden our pitiful feelings concerning ourselves. It's hard to have joy when you don't like the one person you never can get away from—yourself. And we can't really accept the fact that God loves us if we feel He did such a poor job in creating us. Way down deep, some of us believe that we are God's one big mistake. Parents, teachers, schoolmates, associates and the experiences of life seem to confirm our diagnosis.

But we have our facts all wrong. The Bible tells us, "O God, You have declared me perfect in Your eyes" (Psalm 4:1, LB). It also gladly proclaims, "Long ago, even before He made the world, God chose us to be His very own, through what Christ would do for us; He decided then to make us holy in His eyes, without a single fault—we who stand before Him covered with His love" (Ephesians 1:4, LB).

Do you realize that God is not only in the business of declaring us perfect, but in "perfecting us"? (Psalm 138:8) He is changing us from "one degree of glory to another" (II Corinthians 3:18, BERK). Paul doesn't say we are being changed from scum to glory, but from "glory to glory" (KJV).

What a freeing concept to know the magnitude of His love in declaring me perfect and then actually working to make me that way.

If we can accept that, we can accept ourselves in the process. And God knows that I need a whole lot of improvement. I have always been grateful that He doesn't work on 200 things at once in my life. Or 20. But just one thing at a time. Then as I let Him take over that area and work on it, He continues to transform me from that one degree of glory to the next.

We find many little things about ourselves that are hard to accept. One of mine is that I'm a spiller. I spill things. I'm not sure *why* I do—probably I get in too much of a hurry—but anyway, I do. When I finish baking, my kitchen looks as if a tornado had just roared through the room. I am the only person I know who has spilled communion wine on a white suit. And I have done it twice!

God has used my husband to be a human example of His even greater acceptance. Jack just kind of grins with that "so-what-else-is-new-I-love-you-anyhow" grin when I spill something. He has helped me accept myself; and when I spill something now, I can shrug my shoulders and smile. I accept my feelings and my failings much better these days because I see God in my husband's love and acceptance.

And when I can accept myself, that helps me accept others.

It is a psychological principle that our acceptance of others is directly related to how much we accept ourselves.

In my background, "late" was a bad word. Promptness was so ingrained in my childhood that I have trouble being late even if I try. For years, therefore, people who were consistently late were my anathema.

But when I learned to accept myself as one who spills, I found I could accept another who is habitually late.

For me, *joy* in the Christian life depends on (1) delighting in the love letters from God, (2) excitement in seeing God at work daily through answered prayer, (3) acceptance of His great love, and (4) liking myself and accepting myself and others.

Now *that* isn't easy.

In fact, it's impossible.

Impossible, without one further step.

One Saturday I was cleaning house and feeling like the weight of the world was resting right on the top of my head. I was deeply burdened and weary. There was certainly no joy in my life.

I had been thinking about what Christ had said, "Come unto Me, all ye that labor and are heavy laden, and I will give you *rest*" (Matthew 11:28, 29, KJV). I needed that rest.

So I prayed, "Lord, how do I *rest?* My husband doesn't need this heavy-hearted person around. You don't want me to be burdened with the cares of those around me. I am weary of worry. But what can I do?"

Right then a picture focused in my mind:

I was waiting to get on a big, beautiful modern bus, one of the most powerful machines you can imagine. I had a free ticket for an exciting journey. I handed it to the bus driver as I climbed aboard.

The bus was equipped with every comfort—individual, lean-back, rocking-chair type seats with a little table beside each one, and a refrigerator with all kinds of delicious food. Good books and even flowers were available for each passenger.

But as I boarded the bus, I saw some strange people. One man, instead of relaxing in his seat, was standing in the aisle, carrying two heavy suitcases and a back pack on his shoulders. He was perspiring heavily.

When I asked him what he was doing, he replied, "Well, I've been given this wonderful trip absolutely free. I didn't think it was fair that the bus had to carry my bags as well as me, so I am helping out."

After the bus started, I noticed a man jogging in the aisle. He had on a light-weight running suit and was sweating profusely.

I inquired why he was jogging.

He answered, "Well, you see I have been given a trip absolutely free on this bus. But I am not sure it is powerful enough to take us all to our destination, so I am jogging to give it additional power."

Then I spotted a lady in the front. She was sitting on the very edge of her chair, barely perched on the seat and peering over the bus driver's shoulder.

She was the epitome of all the backseat drivers I have ever known. "Watch that pothole!" she exclaimed. "Oohhh, that's a big curve we're coming to. Be careful . . . there's a hill ahead . . . don't go too fast . . . what's over the next hill?" And on and on she went.

Finally the driver stopped the bus and faced us all. His face was kind, strong and gentle. His voice was soft, but firm.

"Dear friends," he said, "we are going on a wonderful journey. Some of it will be through wild and treacherous country, some through beautiful valleys, some through peaceful meadowlands. Your destination far exceeds anything you have ever thought of or dreamed about.

"And I *guarantee* to get you there!

"I have been over this road many times. I know every pothole, every curve, every hill. The bus is so powerful that it cannot break down. The journey is so beautiful and so interesting that I don't want any one of you to miss one moment of it.

"So, friends, why don't you all just sit down and relax."

Then he smiled in the most tender way which softened the rebuke from his words as he concluded, *"And leave the driving to me."*

I sat down and prayed, "Dear Father, I identify with those people on that bus. Sometimes I carry burdens that You have already taken. At times, I must think You don't have the power to get me there. But mostly, I guess, I am like the woman in the front seat. Anxious about the potholes of tomorrow, the mountain of bills, fearful of the next curve. I try to tell *You* how to drive. Or at least try to give You backseat suggestions.

"Oh, Father. Help me relax. Help me enjoy the scenery on this fantastic journey with You. Help me *leave* the driving to You."

That was the secret for me. To *rest* in the strength of God.

Paul says, "Be strong in the *grace* that is in Christ Jesus" (II Timothy 2:1). We need to "be strong," but in what? In His *grace*. Another way to put that would be to say, "Be diligent to *rest*."

God reminds me of this continually as I try to caution Him about some potholes.

The story is told of two Arabs who came to Cairo, Egypt one day and stayed at a modern hotel. They had never been out of the desert before and the thing that fascinated them most was the bathroom water faucet. Instead of going out to explore the city, they stayed in the bathroom all day long, turning the faucet on and off, watching the cool water gush out.

When they went back to their desert homes, they did what they considered to be a smart thing. They unscrewed the water faucet and took it with them.

We may smile at this, but we may be doing the very same thing in our spiritual lives. We think we can have joy without staying in contact with the *Source* of all joy, without being connected to His power, to His love, to His strength.

So rest, and the Source of joy will flow in and through your life as you

- Drink deeply of the water of the Word
- Watch Him work in daily ways through prayer
- Accept His great love
- Accept yourself and others
- And . . . *rest.*

"May He [God] be pleased by all these thoughts about Him, for He is the source of all my joy" (Psalm 104:34, LB).

The Happy Heart/10

The August morning seemed hand-hewn, freshly made just for us. We had been married only two years, and were heading back to Texas for graduate school after a summer in California. Our old car was loaded with everything we owned.

We had two whole days to do anything we wanted, and the spirit of exploration descended upon us. When we saw the sign, "Window Rock, Navajo Reservation" pointing to the right, we simultaneously said, "Let's go!"

We saw Window Rock and were enchanted with the lush valley cradled in the shadows of the jagged mountains, sentineled by birch trees in white unifoms. We seemed to be the sole inhabitants and decided it was too beautiful to leave. Looking at our map, we saw that the gravel road we were traveling paralleled the highway, joining it some miles north. It was tailor-made for us.

And so we began our adventure.

The road narrowed, fording a creek. We had to accelerate

quickly to get the car up the slope on the other side. We had a hollow feeling inside as we realized that from that point on there was no turning back. The road was too narrow to turn around, and the slope on the *other* side of that creek was twice as steep. The car would never make it.

But the autumn morning sparkled, the road was still passable and worry was far from our minds.

The road soon became a tiny cow path, clinging precariously to the edge of a steep mountain. We inched our way over gulleys and rocks feeling like we were hanging out over the sheer cliffs. Obviously, we had taken a wrong turn, but there was no recourse except to keep going.

Rounding a corner, the car hit a giant rock in the road, caving in the oil pan. There was a terrible grinding sound. Jack cut the motor and we sat there in the sudden silence, looking at each other.

We were lost, hungry and scared. No one in the world knew where we were and they wouldn't look for us for days—or even weeks. In my vivid imagination, I saw us torn to pieces by wolves. It would be weeks before our bodies would be found—if ever.

We prayed.

God knew where we were even if we didn't. We locked the car and started walking. From the position of the sun, we felt we must be heading toward the main road.

At the top of every hill, we scanned the horizon for the highway. But every hilltop revealed only another hilltop. The sandals I was wearing were not meant for mountain climbing. Soon big blisters formed on my feet. Jack walked in front of me going downhill so I could put my hands on his shoulders for support. We were hungry, but most of all thirsty. We saw great tracks—perhaps mountain lions—in the dust.

Finally, toward evening, as we came over a hill, we saw the

sun glinting on car windows in the far distance. And immediately before us, on a little rise, was a small Navajo home. Their well gave the best water I ever tasted.

The young Navajo spoke a bit of English and was kind enough to drive us to the highway in his ancient pickup.

From there we tried to hitchhike into Gallup, New Mexico. We were a dirty, dusty, odd-looking couple with no luggage. Cars whizzed by. I really couldn't blame them. I wouldn't have stopped for us either.

Then a small coupe with two elderly ladies rounded the corner. Jack waved them to a stop and asked them for a ride into town. They peered suspiciously at us, and one asked cautiously, "Have you got a gun?"

On being assured that we had no weapons, they graciously took us to Gallup and dropped us off at a hotel across the street from a garage.

The clerk of that hotel did not believe our story for one moment. She probably thought we were a couple of runaway kids, but reluctantly gave us a room after making us pay in advance.

Next morning, Jack and the tow truck driver found that the road we had taken and the one on which we had walked to the highway weren't fit for his truck. They had to drive 125 miles another way in order to reach our car.

We had prayed for our belongings, not terribly valuable, but all we owned. The men at the garage told us that frequently cars were stripped in the town parking lots, and that we should expect to have nothing left when we found our car. When we had been walking to the highway, two truckloads of Indians who spoke no English had passed us heading toward the mountains—and our car—which was blocking the narrow road. They would have a hard time even getting *around* the car and might have to push it aside to get it out of the way. There was nothing to stop them from taking everything removable from our vehicle.

So it was with some anxiety that Jack approached the location where we had abandoned the car. There it was—untouched! Towing it back took most of the day, but fixing it was a matter of minutes. By evening we were on our way to Texas again. We had had our fill of Adventure.

* * *

I learned some things about God that day.

One was that it wasn't just two of His children who were lost on the side of the mountain. It was Jack and Carole Mayhall.

Two individuals.

Persons.

Distinct from any others.

A short time ago as I was reading the Bible, I came across the story of the blind man who was begging on the road to Jericho (Luke 18). He heard a commotion and started asking those around him what all the noise was about. He was told that Jesus of Nazareth was about to pass along the road. So he began to yell as loudly as he could, which must have been very loud because he was heard by Jesus even above the din.

His companions were so embarrassed they told him to be quiet, but that didn't stop *him*. He just kept on yelling at full volume, "Jesus, son of David, have mercy on me!"

This man had discovered that there just *might* be a chance for some help, and he wouldn't quit till he had explored that possibility.

Hundreds must have been crying for help that day. Christ, being God, could have waved His hand and said, "Everyone be healed." *But there is never a crowd with Christ,* only individual people with different hurts and needs and problems. So what did Jesus do?

First, He stopped. In the midst of a busy schedule, surrounded by thousands of people, He stopped. Then He asked that the man be brought over to Him. Why didn't He go over to the man?

Almost always a multitude of people surrounded Christ. When He moved, they moved like a great wave, overflowing everything before them. It might not have been safe for Jesus to have walked over to a blind beggar sitting by the side of the road pleading for help. The man could have been crushed by the crowd.

Christ took the time to have the man brought over to Him. Then He asked a direct question.

"What do you want Me to do for *you?*"

It was obvious to Jesus that the man was blind. He knew his needs and problems. But He asked the man a personal question, which allowed him the freedom to verbalize his own deep need.

The blind man asked for his sight. Prefacing his request with "Lord," he acknowledged that he knew who Christ was, and that He had the power to do what he asked.

Jesus healed him *immediately.*

The formerly blind beggar responded by following Christ and by praising God.

On the mountainside that August day, I learned that there is no "they" with the Lord. The nebulous "they" didn't need finding. Jack and I did.

No crowd for Christ, only individuals with personal, unique needs. It is *my* hurts, *my* fears, *my* problems, *my* heart that are His concern.

And He asks each one of us that wonderful question, "What do you want Me to do for *you?*" Not you *all,* but *you.*

What is the greatest need of my life—of yours? That is where we need to start. Maybe it is a whole new life, a clean slate, a healing of soul. He waits to be asked, because He will never force His will on anyone. But He *is* asking.

The other thing I learned on the mountain was that God doesn't spare us from life's experiences—the pain, the problems, the frustrations. I know God could have made it rain that day so we wouldn't have started out on the side-trip at all. Or He could have prevented us from getting lost. Or hitting that rock.

But He didn't. He did show us, though, how wonderfully He takes care of us, something of how He delivers from fear and a lot of how He protects even our little belongings in answer to prayer. We learned a bit of the reality that David experienced, "Because the Lord is my Shepherd, I have everything I need" (Psalm 23:1, LB). A little boy misquoted it, but was correct when he said, "The Lord is my Shepherd. What more can I want?"

God doesn't promise us complete understanding of all the "whys" of this life, but He does promise us that there *is* an answer and that He will develop our characters through our questions.

This brings peace out of chaos.

Happiness to me is to be *sure* in an unsure world. Happiness is being *real* in a plastic society. Happiness is *security* in the middle of shifting values, shifting conditions and unstable morals.

All of these are centered in the *one* Person of whom it was said, "Jesus Christ is the same yesterday and today, yes and forever" (Hebrews 13:8).

He doesn't promise us *easy living,* but He does promise us *eternal living.* The Bible says, "What happiness for those whose guilt has been forgiven. What joys when sins are covered over! What relief for those who have confessed their sins and God has cleared their record" (Psalm 32:1, LB).

Maybe as you read this, you are feeling lost . . . as if nobody really knows or maybe even cares where you are.

You are lost in a world of confusion, sliding over a cliff of despair, wandering in circles in a marriage from which love has departed. You are tangled in a forest of frustrations and you just don't know where to turn.

You aren't lost to God. He knows *where* you are and is only waiting for you to cry for help. He wants to pick you up in His arms and comfort you and heal you.

Because He loves you.

The Yielded Heart/11

We sat in the car in the spun gold of an October afternoon overlooking the Long Beach harbor. Ships anchored at rest in the shimmering water. A gull drifted overhead.

But the scene was blurred and indistinct.

My husband gently stroked my hair. Futile. I couldn't stop crying.

These were not tears of sorrow. They were born out of frustration and rage.

A few weeks earlier, Jack had told me that his supervisor wanted him to go on a three-and-a-half-week ministry trip. It was our first major separation, and I wasn't looking forward to it. We had been in this new assignment only six months, working with U.S. Navy personnel in a Christian Servicemen's Center and in our home.

To help fill the lonely weeks while Jack would be gone, I had planned to visit my parents in the Midwest with our small daughter.

But as we were sitting in the car that brilliant afternoon,

Jack told me his supervisor didn't think I should go home as both of us should not be away at the same time. It was a decision at which I was mentally screaming.

Out loud I sobbed, "But what possible good can I do here? We are so new. I can't run things even if something does go wrong. I'm no good here without *you!*"

I wasn't angry at Jack. But I was furious with his boss. I thought, *Who does he think he is, anyway, giving me orders? I don't work for him. Jack does. It is a senseless, stupid decision.* Everything in me railed against that decision, and against the man who had made it.

I had a fleeting thought of defying both of them and going home anyway. But truthfully, I was afraid to do that. Not afraid of Jack—though I love him far too much to want to hurt him. Not fear of his supervisor or of putting Jack's job in jeopardy. I was afraid of the consequences of disobeying God.

Back home, I went to my room to "pour it all out" to God. I had the sense to realize that, good attitude or bad, I wasn't going to visit my parents while Jack was gone. In that, I had no choice.

My choice came in whether to have a Dirty Rotten Attitude for three and a half weeks and be bitter, or to give it to God and let Him teach me what I needed to learn through it. I chose the latter.

God is too big to allow someone else's decision to affect His will for my life. God could have abolished the need for Jack's making the trip. He could have caused the supervisor to ask someone else to take it. Or He could have led the boss to change his mind about me staying home. The Bible tells me that the hearts of *kings* are in the hands of God (Proverbs 8:15). He can certainly control one small supervisor.

I was forced to say, "All right, Lord, I guess it really isn't Jack's superior that I'm mad at. It is You. Because You allowed this to happen. Only I don't want to be mad at You. I know You only do things that are good for me. You do 'all things well.' So teach me in this what it is You want me to learn."

And what a month that was. Loneliness for Jack, certainly. But a heart winged with peace.

Later, I had the opportunity to see God's delightful *timing*. In visiting my parents a few months later, I discovered that at the time of my originally scheduled visit, Mom had been in the hospital. I hadn't been told to spare me worry. But at the time I did go home, we were able to have a beautiful visit. I also had the privilege of attending a wedding of dear friends and an Easter conference in magnificent Colorado. Bonuses from God. Prepared in His timing.

I needed to learn to hold my husband with a very loose grip. Jack is only loaned to me. I don't own him—God does. And any time God wants Jack's entire time and attention, I have no right to try to withhold it.

But God still needed to hammer the lid down on that lesson.

Jack had been back two days, and we were eagerly looking forward to his day off. A packed week made Tuesday the only likely day for some needed time together. On Monday the supervisor called. He was having an *all-day meeting* the next day, and my husband had to be there.

Did I stay calm, cool and rejoicing? Not for a moment! All the anger and frustration I had felt before rolled over me in waves of resentment.

This time it didn't take God quite so long to break through my mental rantings. "Carole," He seemed to say, "did you mean it? Is Jack *really* Mine?"

Yes. He was.

So I gave up. I let go and let God take over.

God is not a grudging giver. He is a God who delights to give us the "desires of our hearts." Many times after He has been a faithful *teacher,* He turns right around and gives us the very thing He was withholding in *order* to teach us.

Only two days later, God loosened our tight schedule, and we shared a deeply satisfying day, made more precious by the lessons learned from God. You see, it isn't that God doesn't want me to *have* the time with my husband. But He does want me to be willing *not* to have it—for Him.

I still struggle with this. And God continues to ask me two vital questions: (1) Do I really believe that God is in control of every circumstance that enters my life? (2) Have I really given my husband, including my husband's *time,* to God?

All too often, we allow bitterness and resentment to creep into so many areas of our lives. Let's suppose your husband was demoted in his job because of an unfair boss. Do you blame the boss or do your really believe God had allowed it for a reason?

Can anything touch us that God has not ordained? Remember that He "upholds all things by the word of His power" (Hebrews 1:3). In reality, if we get bitter at people who demand unfairly or treat us shamefully or abuse our loved ones, on whom are we laying the blame? God.

The Bible states strongly, "See to it that no one comes short of the grace of God; that no root of bitterness springing up causes trouble, and by it many be defiled" (Hebrews 12:15).

I am learning that when bitterness gets a stranglehold on me, it is extremely difficult to get rid of it. So the moment God reveals to me that I *am* bitter about something or someone, I bring it to Him and confess it. John says, "If we confess our sins, He is faithful and righteous to forgive us our sins and to cleanse us from all unrighteousness" (I John 1:9). Bitterness is especially terrible because it is not only a sin against God, but it also has tentacles which wind themselves about our souls and squeeze all the joy from our lives.

Forgiveness and cleansing result from confession—first of all to God; then at times to the person against whom I have been bitter as well.

When I have been deeply gripped by bitterness, a further step I needed was to ask the Lord to literally "create in me a *clean* heart . . . and renew a steadfast spirit within me" (Psalm 51:10).

Bitterness comes from real or supposed injustices and has no place in the life of a Christian. We cannot allow the acid of bitterness to eat away the fabric of our joy and peace. God IS. And He is in control. When the heart is yielded to His control, all is at peace.

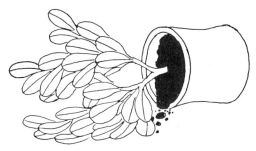

The Wounded Heart/12

I put the key in the ignition quickly, for Jack was waiting on crutches at the hospital entrance for me to pick him up. As I turned the key, the entire lock caved in and disappeared behind the dashboard.

I wavered between hysterical laughter and tears.

It was a larger, borrowed car because Jack's leg cast wouldn't fit into our VW. I hastily found a screwdriver, scraped a hole in the cardboard glove compartment, pushed the lock into place with my right hand and turned the key with my left. The car started.

What more could go wrong? Only everything.

Those weeks were a kaleidoscope of frustrations. Jack had severed his knee ligaments in a skiing accident, and a surgeon had stitched them together. A few days after Jack came home from the hospital, he suddenly had severe pains in his arm and heart. Something serious had happened. We raced through the streets, sirens wailing, as the ambulance took us to the hospital. Doctors and nurses rushed about looking grave. Two hours later, our doctor explained that a blood clot had broken loose from the knee, raced through Jack's heart and lodged in his lung.

Fortunately I had no idea how really serious that was till a doctor friend told us later that we should get down on our knees and thank God three times a day that Jack was alive.

But at the time I only knew that Jack looked white and weak on the hospital bed.

A week later, when our hopes were high for his release, a slight overmedication to prevent further clots caused the knee wound to break open. Blood saturated the cast. Infection set in.

Just when the heart doctor had said Jack could go home, the leg doctor now said he had to stay. When the leg doctor finally released him, the heart doctor said he wasn't stabilized yet.

Meanwhile, I wasn't coping too well. Our five-year-old daughter was violently ill and became hysterical when I would leave to visit Jack. In taking a sickbed tray to her one evening, I put it down for a moment on the kitchen counter. It overturned, tipping all its contents onto the already sticky floor. The washing machine had been leaking several gallons of water all over the kitchen floor on every rinse cycle.

Big things, too. My father had died of leukemia in the spring of that year, which caused Mother to become ill and enter the hospital. We had no money for our growing hospital and doctor bills, accumulating quickly from Jack's accident.

I wasn't used to facing these things without the support of Jack, who always before had blunted the hard edge of the problems we faced together.

I clung to the fact that nothing is accidental or incidental with God.

"But, O God." I prayed, "You must be trying to get

through to me on a *very* great lesson this time. I'd like to ask You to let up a bit. But in a deeper part of me, I don't want You to let up till I've learned completely. I surely don't want to have to relearn *this* one by going through *another* such time as this."

I learned many lessons through those weeks as God continued to take care of us. When Jack was *finally* released from the hospital, I knew he couldn't leave till we had paid the bill or at least made some arrangements to pay it. Those weeks had been so frantic, I hadn't given much thought to financing this nightmare. Praying for God to work it all out *somehow,* I gathered up every cent I could find in the house—Jack's paycheck, some checks from concerned friends, grocery money, loose change. I stuffed it all into my purse. It wasn't till I reached the accounting office and the bill was handed to me, that I counted what was there. I had the exact amount with 27¢ left over!

But God had a much more pointed message than again showing us the miracle of His provision. It was the lesson of "The Thankful Heart."

God had begun this lesson the day Lynn spilled that can of paint all over the kitchen floor two years earlier. Now He was distilling it for me.

Often I pray that I will learn these lessons from God quickly. It isn't only out of a desire to please Him that I ask it. It is also because I don't want to have to learn the hard way.

The first time children do something wrong, we speak softly in correcting them. The second, more firmly. The third admonition may be more directly applied.

God is our perfect parent. He is faithful to teach us when we learn easily, when we resist stubbornly or when the lesson needs to be redefined and deepened in our lives.

During those months, it seemed that everything that could

go wrong, did. God didn't let up till I had learned the lesson "by heart"—to be thankful *in everything*. In frustrations. In sickness. In "accidents" and circumstances I could not comprehend. Whenever. Whatever. Whoever. All the time.

During this period God gave me some glimmerings as to why it is so important to have a thankful spirit.

A heart of praise pleases God. It is a "sacrifice" to Him (Hebrews 13:15). When everything is right with our world, it is no sacrifice for us to be thankful. But when a part of our world is coming apart at the seams it *is* a sacrifice to praise God. We sacrifice our self-pity. We sacrifice others' pity too. We may have to sacrifice the black mood we have wrapped around ourselves so protectingly.

When we are thankful and offer Him this sacrifice, our hearts change from grumpiness to being grateful, from complaining to being gracious.

"But how come so *much,* Lord?" I persisted. "So many things for so long. Why?" No answer was forthcoming . . . then.

Later I did get further insight into the "why" of giving thanks for all the little strange events that take place. If I do not learn to give thanks in seemingly insignificant and incomprehensible events, how will I ever develop the habit of life with the strength and courage it takes, to really give thanks when major things happen?

My sister had told me of a young man whose wife, son and mother-in-law were in an automobile accident. The father-in-law called the man to tell him about it. He said, "Son, there's been an accident involving my wife, your wife and your little boy. Your wife and mine are all right, but your little boy was taken to be with God."

The man's immediate response was, "Praise the Lord!"

When I heard about this, I thought, *How could it be? How could he possibly say that immediately? That's unreal.*

I couldn't do it. Perhaps a year later I could reflect that going to be with God, to live and grow up in a perfect environment was the best thing for that little boy. Maybe even a month later I could face this, knowing that God had to be in control. But immediately? No.

I realize that God gives special grace in times of special need. And He doesn't give it to us till we *do* need it.

I also began to see that unless I learn to turn to God and say, "Thank You, God. I don't understand this fiery furnace that I am in right now, but I thank You anyhow," in the dailies of life, I will never be able to give thanks for the rocks and hard places of life that await every one of us.

We are to thank Him *in* everything (I Thessalonians 5:18) and *for* everything (Ephesians 5:20). We have no "out."

But then, why shouldn't we give Him the sacrifice of our praise? Our God, the great God of the universe, is *for* us.

"What then shall we say to these things? If God is for us, who is against us?" (Romans 8:31)

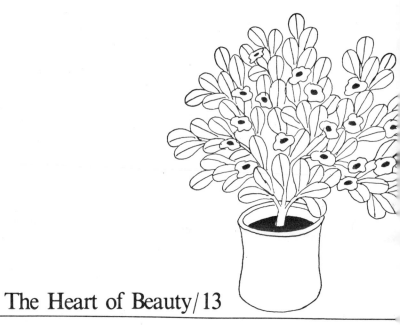

The Heart of Beauty/13

The model stood poised, her slim figure reflected by the floor-length mirror behind her. She had been speaking to a group of wives on the "secrets of beauty," and I was squirming inside.

In less than 30 minutes I had found out I wasn't walking correctly, my posture leaves much to be desired and I was a few pounds overweight. I didn't like the reminder.

I can still remember a day when, at the age of 13, I looked into a mirror and burst into tears. When Mother asked what was the matter, I sobbed mournfully, "Oh, Mother, I am so *ugly!*" And none of us want to be ugly.

"Beauty is in the eye of the beholder" is a true axiom. To one person, beauty is graciousness. To another, it is a quality of face and figure that is pleasing to the eye. To another, it radiates from an inner fragrance of loveliness.

The dictionary defines beauty as "the quality or aggregate of qualities in a person or thing that gives pleasure to the senses or pleasurably exalts the mind or spirit: loveliness."

The first part of that definition, "pleasurable to the senses," is what the American woman spends over two billion dollars a year on—cosmetics to make her look, feel and smell beautiful. And most of us seem willing to work at making the most of whatever the Lord gave us. I expect to be working at that the rest of my life.

But the other part of that definition is "the quality that pleasurably exalts the mind or spirit." And *that* is something else again.

I met a woman the other day who was somewhat plump. Her wispy hair was held in place with a bobby pin; her nose was slightly too large for her face. But as I talked to her, a deep loveliness shone through; and I went away from her thinking, *What a beautiful person.*

That's the kind of beauty I long for.

Sometimes a person can start out ugly, then become beautiful. Sometimes a person can be beautiful, then grow into something ugly. No one can help not being pretty at 20. But it may be her own fault if she is not pretty at 40.

Many things hinder us from becoming beautiful outwardly. Some we cannot control. The woman who has been forced to work so hard that her health is broken may be old before her time, but she can still be beautiful.

As I started thinking about what can hinder us from inner beauty, I realized that some things are like acid eating away at a lovely skin.

Worry is one of these.

Now I am a pretty good worrier. A friend of mine convicted me of this when she said, "My mother said she trusted in God, but she *worried* all the time."

I can preach sermons on the fact that worry and trust are totally incompatible. But let *my* daughter be two hours late in a terrible storm, let *my* husband be overseas and no communication for a week, let *my* friend's children be breaking her heart, and what do I do?

Well, I get *concerned.* After all, isn't a Christian supposed to show concern? Aren't we supposed to "bear one another's burdens"?

I cannot excuse myself by calling worry "concern."

One of my favorite verses in the Psalms is: "I sought the Lord, and He answered me, and delivered me from *all my fears"* (34:4).

Fear cannot help but hinder us from the command of the next verse which says, "Look to Him and be *radiant."*

My niece sent her mother the following poem from college:

From "Cain became very angry and his countenance fell"
(Genesis 4:5).

One cannot be angry
and radiant.

Perhaps I have cause to be angry.
Perhaps I have been honestly wronged.
Perhaps I am entirely innocent.
Perhaps . . .
Well,
    but not very likely.
But even if I were entirely innocent,
would my anger be fitting?
What would it accomplish?
Would not that anger smoldering in my heart
        deaden the radiance of my face?
    . and should not the face of one
        in whom God dwells have a radiance?

But I *have* been wronged!

Is this a cause for happiness?
Christian happiness does not need a cause.
It needs only to be freed of obstruction,
    and it will shine."

Years ago I read an article on "The Perfect Wife" in a
national magazine, and it had this to say:

> One man said of his wife, "To tell the truth I sometimes see
> her as ugly. Not because of how she's dressed or made up. I see
> her as ugly when she sounds ugly."
>
> He was by no means the only husband to point out that his
> wife was far prettier when she was not scolding, then when she
> was. In other words, before one is married, beauty might be
> strictly in the eye of the beholder, but afterwards it tends to be
> in his ear.

An amusing poem I read recently said:

> When people disagree with me,
> My argument's not strong.
> I grant their sacred right to be
>   knotheaded, blind and wrong!

Solomon reminds me that my mouth is to be a "well of
life" (Proverbs 10:11, KJV). Hostility and anger are not com-
patible with a mouth which is a "well of life."

Inner beauty is really my being a clean mirror to reflect
Christ. Worry, anger, hostility and bitterness cloud and film
that mirror. It takes the polishing of the Holy Spirit, the
cleansing of the Word and the diligence of obedience for that
mirror to be kept clean.

The key is obedience.

Someone has suggested that the way to spell "abide" with
four letters is "o-b-e-y." In order to abide deeply in Christ, to
experience His joy, to really reflect Him in our lives and have
inner beauty of heart and character, we have to *obey*.

The psalmist says, "I thought on my ways, and turned my

feet unto Thy testimonies. I *made haste,* and delayed not to keep Thy commandments" (Psalm 119:59, 60, KJV).

A friend told how he practiced this. As soon as he reads a command in the Bible, he obeys it at the *first available* opportunity. If he is reading the Psalms and the passage says to sing a joyful song unto the Lord, he stops right then to sing. If it says to let his heart be full of praise, he begins praising God. If it says to tell others about Christ, the next person he meets is the one he'll talk to.

Now that's a heart tuned in to God's signals, sensitive to His messages and obedient to the voice of the living God.

When I was taking tennis lessons, I was shown how to follow through on my backhand. The value of following through was demonstrated, explained and shown to me. My problem comes in *doing* it. All that training can't help me if I don't *do* what I know to do. Sometimes I think, *If I had the pro at my elbow every minute, maybe I'd be able to practice this correctly.*

In obeying God's rules, we not only have the Instructor at our elbow, we have Him dwelling in us—to give us the ability, the desire, the strength to *obey* His commands. We are without excuse when we fail.

I'm glad God never loses patience. He forgives our failures, and we start with a fresh slate. But we'll never get proficient in living this Christian life if we don't put His instructions into practice.

God's Word is negated if not obeyed.

It would not have helped me to study the Bible, to listen to God in prayer, to hear the Word taught, to read it or memorize it or meditate on it. None of these ways of knowing God would have helped me grow one bit if I had refused to *do* the things He told me.

God does not want us to play games in the spiritual realm. He warns, "If you love Me, *keep* My commandments" (Jonn

14:15, KJV); and, "You are My friends, if you *do* what I command you" (John 15:14).

Christ reveals Himself to us as we obey. He says, "He who has My commandments and keeps them, he it is who loves Me; and he who loves Me shall be loved by My Father, and I will love him, and will *disclose Myself to him*" (John 14:21).

God wants my life—your life—to be an Adventure with a capital *A*. He wants to be our constant companion. He has given . . . He is giving . . . He *will* give untold riches and unending experiences. He requires but one thing—obedience.

God *will* show Himself to us. He *will* touch us again and again with His hands of love. He *will* make us beautiful.

He *will* enable us to *see* Him. Clearly. Distinctly.

Obey Him. It will be . . . the beginning.